Dedicated

To my mother, whose love for
writing and books
we both share.

TABLE OF CONTENTS

CATALOG

Legal Tender

Tokens

GUIDEBOOK

Dates, Mintmarks, Numbers Issued, Minted or Printed, and Values of the Legal Tender and Token Coins and Notes

THE CATALOG AND GUIDEBOOK OF SOUTHEAST ASIAN COINS AND CURRENCY

VOLUME I

FRANCE

BY

HOWARD A. DANIEL, III

SECOND EDITION

Photography by Buddy King, Rodney M. George, Jr. and Joseph E. Boling

FIRST EDITION
One Printing (100 copies), October 1975

SECOND EDITION
One Printing (1,000 copies), December 1978

BNR Press

Box 157
Portage, Ohio 43451

Box 9
Camden, South Carolina 29020

Library of Congress Catalog Number
78-60307

ISBN 0-931960-01-0

Printed in the United States of America

PREFACE

This second edition is extensively revised but it is not perfect or complete. The existence of some coins and notes is still unknown or doubtful. Sources mention them, but many have not been confirmed to the numismatic community known to me. The next edition will include more descriptions about the proofs, patterns and specimens of circulating coins, notes and tokens. Please do not consider any item in your collection or library not appearing in this book to be too trivial. Your new lower or higher block and serial number, city of issue, date, mintmark, measurements, etc., can be a significant contribution about a particular coin or note. Every piece of new data, rubbing, photograph or photocopy completes the picture that much more for your fellow collectors and readers. I am searching for the complete truth, but it cannot be reached without the assistance of readers like yourself. If you know of any errors, omissions or corrections, please contact me directly or through the BNR Press.

My wife Phung has again assisted and encouraged me, even when it meant adjusting our budget and time together. Christopher C. Currie's original, and continuing, correspondence still makes up the majority of information about Indochina coins. Anton Fox has also greatly assisted me with additional data about Cochinchina and Indochina coins and tokens. David B. August's personal collection and information has been of tremendous assistance in the area of bank notes. A very informative visit with Albert Pick made me realize that many more years of studying are necessary for me to approach his vast knowledge about paper money. Joseph E. Boling, Mrs. Adolph B. Hill, Jr., and Clyde M. Reedy have also made significant paper money contributions. Some contributors have their employers or offices added to their names. Even though some acted in their private capacity, they may have been inhibited to contribute, if their employer or organization did not support numismatic research. Also I especially want to thank the dealers (some operate under their own names) and their employees that patiently allowed me to research their stock by mail and over the counter. You couldn't find a better group of people to give your business. I wish more could be written about each contributor, but the acknowledgments must be limited to one page in this edition. Hope you enjoy the book.

Howard A. Daniel, III

CONTRIBUTORS

David B. August

Erwin Beyer

Joseph E. Boling

Colin R. Bruce, II
(of Krause Publications)

Francis D. Campbell, Jr.
(Librarian of ANS)

Dr. Steven Carol

Daniel K.E. Ching

Henry Christensen

Christopher C. Currie

Paul Curtis
(President and Auctioneer of the World Paper Currency Collectors)

Richard G. Doty
(Associate Curator of Modern Coins, ANS)

Wilhelm R. Eglseer

Joe Elliott
(of Fred Sweeney Rare Coins, Inc.)

Anton F. Fox

Chester J. Frear

Victor Gadoury

Melvin P. Hennisch, M.D.

William G. Henderson

Mrs. Adolph B. Hill, Jr.
(IBNS Honorary Director for Life)

Patrick D. Hogan
(Librarian of ONS, SON and WPCC)

Granvyl G. Hulse, Jr.
(Librarian of NI)

John G. Humphris

Carl H. Jaeschke
(Museum Specialist at Smithsonian)

Geneva Karlson
(Librarian of ANA)

Richard A. Kelly

Brian Kemp
(of Stanley Gibbons Currency, Ltd.)

Joseph L. Lepczyk

James Lorah

C.M. Nielsen

George S. Notarpole

Roger Outing

Carol Plante

Jess Peters

Albert Pick
(Curator of Bayerische Hypotheken und Wechsel Bank Collection)

Clyde M. Reedy

Hans M.F. Schulman
(formerly of Schulman Coin & Mint, Inc.)

C. Frederick Schwan
(of BNR Press)

Scott Semans

Bruce W. Smith
(of Point Coin & Stamp and formerly of Krause Publications)

Gary F. Snover

Mrs. Susan R. J. Stuart
(of Stanley Gibbons Currency, Ltd.)

Clarence J. Symes
(of Danny Boy Enterprises)

CATALOG INTRODUCTION

The Catalog has two major sections. One describes the legal tender coins and notes and the other the token coins and notes. Within each section the coins and notes are grouped by country, colony or protectorate. These are preceded by maps, numismatic and economic history, and related information. The coins and notes are merged together in sequence by date of issue to demonstrate their close relationship. Most catalog pages are followed by photographs or drawings of the major types and some varieties. The catalog pages have the following information:

Government/Dynasty: The government name or dynasty name within which the coin or note circulated.

Governor/Minister/King: The individual's name at the head of the government or dynasty.

Chief of State/Reign Title: The individual's name at the head of the local state or government under the governor or king, or the reign title of the king.

Minted/Printed At: The place name and, if known, the name of the government or private agency of manufacture. Some mintmarks will follow the names in parenthesis when more than one appears within a series of coins or notes.

Mint Director: The individual's name that directed the mint.

Designer: The individual's name that designed a coin or note.

Engraver: The individual's name that engraved a coin or note.

Dates of Issue: The earliest and latest dates of issue for all the coins or notes on a page. Within each country, colony or protectorate the coins and notes are in sequence according to the earliest date of issue.

Cty, Code & Number: The Country(Cty), colony and protectorate abbreviations used are as follows:

FC: French Cochinchina	IF: Indies, Neth. East(French)	VF: Viet Nam, French
FI: French Indochina	KF: Khmer(Cambodia), French	TF: Thailand(French)
	LF: Laos, French	

The Type Code(Code) abbreviations are as follows:

C : Coin, Legal Tender	CT: Coin, Token	N : Note, Legal Tender
CF: Coin, Foreign		NT: Note, Token

The catalog number(Number) starts with number 1 within each of the country and type codes. Lower case letters following the catalog number designate varieties of the type. The catalog number could be preceded by the following upper case letters for further indentification:

F : Fake/Counterfeit	H : Holed(not originally, but later by legal authority)	S : Specimen/Proof
		U : Specimen, Unissued

This scheme will be expanded as required for use with succeeding volumes. This system has been used successfully in recording, locating and sorting data about a coin or note as well as related background information. For identification on holders, catalogs, price lists, etc., if the country and type code are known or described, they may be dropped. The catalog number could be used as Daniel 4e, Dan S4, D-5 or D-U38.

Denomination: The denominations and their relationships are as follows:

1000 Sapeques(holed 1 Centime) = 8 Reales(1 Piastre) = 1 Dollar, French Cochinchina 1862 - 1879
500 Sapeques = 100 Cents = 1 Piastre, French Cochinchina and Indochina 1879 - 1905
400 Centimes = 4 Francs, French Cambodia c1880 - 1905
600 Sapeques = 100 Cents = 1 Piastre, French Indochina 1905 - 1914
100 Cents = 1 Piastre, French Indochina 1914 - 1954
100 Cents(Sen) = 1 Piastre(Riel), French Cambodia 1952 - 1954
100 Cents(Att) = 1 Piastre(Kip), French Laos 1952 - 1954
100 Cents(Xu) = 1 Piastre(Dong), French Viet Nam 1952 - 1954

The use of *Su* on Vietnamese coins is the phonetic spelling of the word *Xu* for cents.

Diameter(mm), Thickness(mm), Weight(gram), Width(mm) and Length(mm): Self-explanatory.

Metal: The major metal of a coin is listed in the column. The narrative line describes the complete composition of the metal, if known, using 1.00 as the whole.

Major Color: The major or most distinguishing printed color of the face side of a note is listed. Aside from values this is the next most controversial part of this volume.

Edge: Coin edges are described as smooth, reeded, or security.

Signatures: Signatures are numbered and listed from left to right as they are printed on the note. Most signature combinations are illustrated in the photographs or drawings on the pages immediately following their description. The Signature Chart at page 127 illustrates all of the numbered signatures.

Rarity: Few collections or dealer's stocks are completely identified by the engravers, signatures, varieties, etc., described in this volume. As more of these coins and notes are completely identified rarity numbers may decrease for some, but it is very probable that even rarer varieties will be discovered. The rarity is based on the number of pieces reported and known to the author and are described as follows:

Rarity 9. 1 - 3 known
Rarity 8. 4 - 10(extremely rare)
Rarity 7. 11 - 24(very rare)
Rarity 6. 25 - 49(rare)
Rarity 5. 50 - 99(extremely scarce)
Rarity 4. 100 - 199(very scarce)
Rarity 3. 200 - 299(scarce)
Rarity 2. 300 - 499(uncommon)
Rarity 1. 500 or more(common)

Paper: Printing paper is identified as thin, medium or thick.

Mintmark: The mintmark or lack of one is listed. The abbreviation Tb is used for the Thunderbolt symbol of the Poissy Mint, France.

Mint Director's Sign: The sign or lack of one is listed for the individual that directed the mint.

Engraver's Sign: The sign or lack of one is listed for the individual that engraved a coin.

Watermark: The watermark or lack of one is indicated. Some denominations or catalog numbers will follow in parenthesis when more than one appears within a series of notes.

Obverse and Reverse; Face and Back: Coin and note descriptions are combined as much as possible to further describe unique areas of designs. A complete description can usually be assembled by combining descriptions at each variety. Every attempt has been made to acquire drawings or photographs of every item and to illustrate them in sizes large enough to distinguish all major features. There are some additional descriptions and interpretations about coins and notes within the numismatic and economic history, and related information preceding each country, colony or protectorate.

FRENCH COCHINCHINA

1859-1885

During the reign of Napoleon III, a Franco-Spanish squadron under the command of Admiral Rigault de Genouilly captured Saigon on 18 February 1859. A French naval expeditionary force under the command of Admiral Bonard was established to occupy Saigon and the close surrounding territory. On 10 April 1862, he decreed that the Mexican Piastre (8 Reales) would be legal tender. Change was made by dividing the coin into one-fourth, one-eighth, and one-half pieces. The native zinc, copper, silver and gold coins and bars of Southeast Asia and China were also used when the supply of legal tender coins could not meet the demand.

Within two years after capturing Saigon, French influence spread out to the eastern provinces and the Mekong Delta. By June 1862, Admiral Bonard conquered the three eastern provinces, Bien Hoa, Gia Dinh and My Tho, and signed a treaty with the Vietnamese which ceded them to France. Admiral Lagrandiere, Admiral Bonard's successor, went to the Cambodian capital of Oudon in 1863 and signed a Treaty of Protectorate with King Norodom I. This treaty prevented the conquest and division of Cambodia by Viet Nam and Siam (Thailand). Since 1862 the three western provinces, Ha Tien, Chau Doc, and Vinh Long, were separated from the rest of Viet Nam. The Vietnamese residents were causing problems for the French that the local government would not suppress. Admiral Lagrandiere annexed the provinces in 1867 with French troops eliminating all resistance.

The budget and finances of the region were compiled in French Francs, even though the Mexican Piastre was legal tender and the most common coin of the entire Far East. In 1864, Admiral Lagrandiere decreed the French Ecu(5 Francs) to be valued at 90% of an Mexican Piastre in an attempt to create a French Franc currency system for Cambodia and Cochinchina. The French Ecu's legal value was then 3% lower than its intrinsic value, thus causing them to disappear into the melting pot and the decree was quickly revoked. There is an indication that some of the French Ecus were still in circulation in Cambodia when the French Franc coinage of King Norodom I was introduced in about 1880.

The decree of 25 January 1875 authorized the establishment of a privately capitalized bank with the monopoly of issuing bank notes. Some far-sighted individual named it the Banque de l'Indochine(Bank of Indochina) with its headquarters in Paris and a branch office in Saigon. Branches were later established in other cities of Cochinchina. The first series of bank notes was printed by the Bank of France and issued in 5, 20 and 100 Dollars(Piastres) denominations from 1876 to approximately 1891 with a total of 12 million dollars placed into circulation.

The last attempt to put French Franc type coins in circulation was the issue of the French 1 Centime of 1875 with the K(Bordeaux) mintmark in 1878. One million of these coins were imported and a 3 millimeter hole was punched in the center at the Saigon Arsenal. Their legal value was put at 1000 to the Dollar and they were named Sapeques(FC CF H1), which is also the French name for the Vietnamese round coins with square holes. These holed 1 Centime coins were almost completely rejected by the Vietnamese and were very shortly withdrawn from circulation.

FC CF H1

The decree of 24 December 1878 established a study group to design acceptable French coins. The decrees of 7 and 22 April 1879 created the designs, denominations, metals, and weights of the Sapeque(1/5 Cent), 1 Cent, 10 Cents, 20 Cents, 50 Cents, and Piastre. The Governor-General authorized the issue of all the coins, except the Piastre, and allowed the Mexican Piastre and other foreign dollar-size coins to continue in circulation. No circulation strikes, only patterns and proofs, were ever minted of the Cochinchina Piastre. The Vietnamese (Chinese-style) characters on the reverse of the Sapeque are written as two parts of a thousand, when its value was placed at one part of five hundred of a Piastre! The confusion must be related to the Sapeque of 1878 which weighed and was valued at half the 1879 Sapeque? During this period, the territory under the control of the French naval expeditionary force, minus Cambodia, was formed into the French Colony of Cochinchina with a civilian Governor-General at its head in Saigon. The Resident-Superior at Phnom Penh, the new capital in the Protectorate of Cambodia, was placed under the control of the Governor-General.

The French explored the lands north of Cochinchina and Cambodia. An expeditionary force in north Viet Nam created a chain of events which ended Viet Nam's independence with treaties signed on 25 August 1883 and 6 June 1884. In 1885 the Chinese withdrew all claims of allegiance and the silver seal conferred on the Emperor of Viet Nam was melted. The gaining of the new territory forced the creation of a French administration to govern the Protectorates of Annam(central Viet Nam), Tonkin(north Viet Nam), Cambodia, and the Colony of Cochinchina. The new administration was named French Indochina with Residents-Superior added in Hanoi and Hue. The name was changed to Indochina on all 1885 dated coins, except 1 Cents were struck for Cochinchina and Indochina.

FRENCH COCHINCHINA NOTE — LEGAL TENDER

SERIES 1875

Government: Colony of Cochinchina and Protectorate of Cambodia

Governor: Rear Admiral Baron Victor-Auguste Duperre

Printed at: Bank of France, Paris, France

Designer: A. Bramtot and Georges Duval

Engraver: Ch. Wullschleger and J. Robert

Dates of Issue: 1876 - 1891

cty, code & number	denomination	width	length	major color	signatures	rarity
FC N 1a	5 Dollars	94mm	181mm	Blue	1	8
1b		94	181	Blue	1	9
FC N 2a	20 Dollars	118	207	Blue	1	8
2b		118	207	Blue	1	9
FC N 3a	100 Dollars	145	215	Blue	1	8
3b		145	215	Blue	1	9

Paper: Thin White

Watermark: Head of Mercury

Face: 5-100D: BANQUE DE L'INDOCHINE in one line top center or top right(20D) center with DECRET DU 21 JANVIER 1875 above and printed SAIGON(a) or HAIPHONG overstamped on SAIGON(b) with handwritten date below. A-BRAMTOT ET G.DUVAL.FEC. in lower left and CH-WULLSCHLEGER.SC. or J.ROBERT SC.(100D) in lower right margins. 5D: FIVE DOLLARS center and CINQ PIASTRES right. Watermark circle upper left and seated Neptune left. 20D: TWENTY DOLLARS left center and VINGT PIASTRES right. Elephants standing in front of columns left and right. Stand with potted plant atop at bottom center of the note with French woman and cow left and Indian woman and tiger right. Watermark area at center. 100D: ONE HUNDRED DOLLARS left and CENT PIASTRES right. Vasco de Gama standing in front of column left and Oriental male right. Ships and boats bottom center.

Back: 5-100D: Various designs with open areas for Vietnamese(Chinese-style) characters describing the notes as issues of the Bank of Indochina in the colony of Cochinchina, their denomination and that they are payable in silver, and the counterfeiting Article 139 in French.

FRENCH COCHINCHINA NOTE — LEGAL TENDER
SERIES 1875

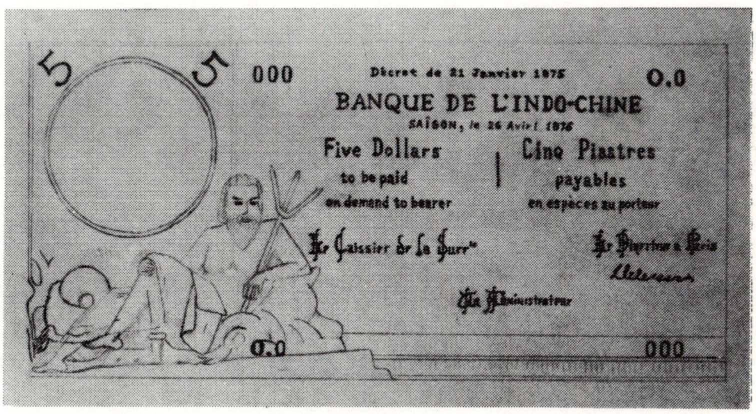

FC N 1a

Author's conception and drawing of 5 Dollars note.

FRENCH COCHINCHINA COIN — LEGAL TENDER

SERIES 1879

Government: Colony of Cochinchina and Protectorate of Cambodia

Governor: Charles Le Myre de Vilers

Minted at: Paris Mint, France

Mint Director: Renouard de Bussiere (Moth) and Jean Ruau (Horn)

Designer: Auguste Barre

Engraver: Auguste Barre (Anchor) and Jean Lagrange (Fasces)

Dates of Issue: 2 August 1879 - 1885

cty, code & number	denomination	diameter	thickness	weight	metal	edge	rarity
FC C 1	Sapeque (1/5Cent)	20.0mm	.75mm	2.03 grams	Bronze	Smooth	1
FC C 2	1 Cent	31.0	1.75	10.0	Bronze	Smooth	2
FC C 3	10 Cents	19.0	1.0	2.721	Silver	Reeded	2
FC C 4	20 Cents	26.0	2.0	5.443	Silver	Reeded	2
FC C 5	50 Cents	29.0	2.0	13.607	Silver	Reeded	3

Metal: Bronze (.85 copper and .15 tin) and Silver (.90 and .10 copper)

Mintmark: A **Mint Director's Sign:** Moth or Horn **Engraver's Sign:** Anchor or Fasces

Obverse: S: COCHINCHINE FRANCAISE around top edge. Date bottom edge, mintmark above, Mint Director's sign left and Engraver's right. 4.5mm square hole center. 1-50C: REPUBLIQUE FRANCAISE around top edge. Symbolic figure of France seated and holding fasces, anchor behind and grain standing before. 1C: A.B bottom right under France, mintmark bottom center, and straight and beaded circles around. Date bottom edge with Mint Director's sign left and Engraver's right. 10-50C: Date bottom edge with BARRE left.

Reverse: S: Eight Vietnamese(Chinese-style) characters around square hole meaning (two parts of thousand) one-fifth cent. 1C: COCHINCHINE FRANCAISE around top edge and POIDS 10 GR at bottom edge. Rectangle in horizontal position around four Vietnamese(Chinese-style) characters meaning (one part of hundred) one cent. 1 to left and C right of rectangle with beaded circle around all. 10-50C: COCHINCHINE FRANCAISE around top edge and wreath of leaves and berries around center area tied with a ribbon at the base. At top of base is the mintmark with Mint Director's sign left and Engraver's right, and denomination in two lines in center. 10C: TITRE 0.900. POIDS 2,721, 20C: 5,443, and 50C: 13,607 GR. around bottom edge.

FRENCH COCHINCHINA COIN — LEGAL TENDER

SERIES 1879

FC C 1

FC C 2

FC C 3

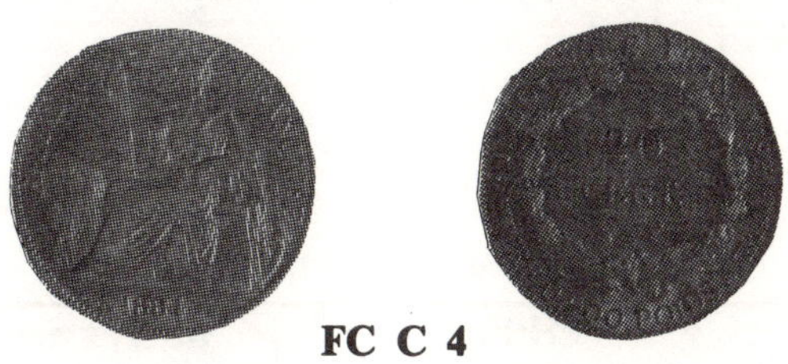

FC C 4

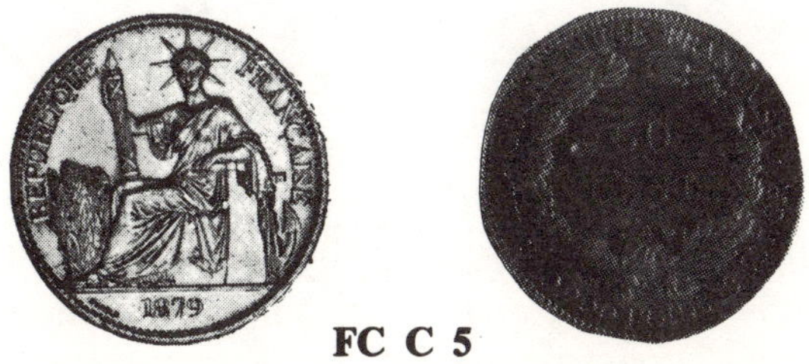

FC C 5

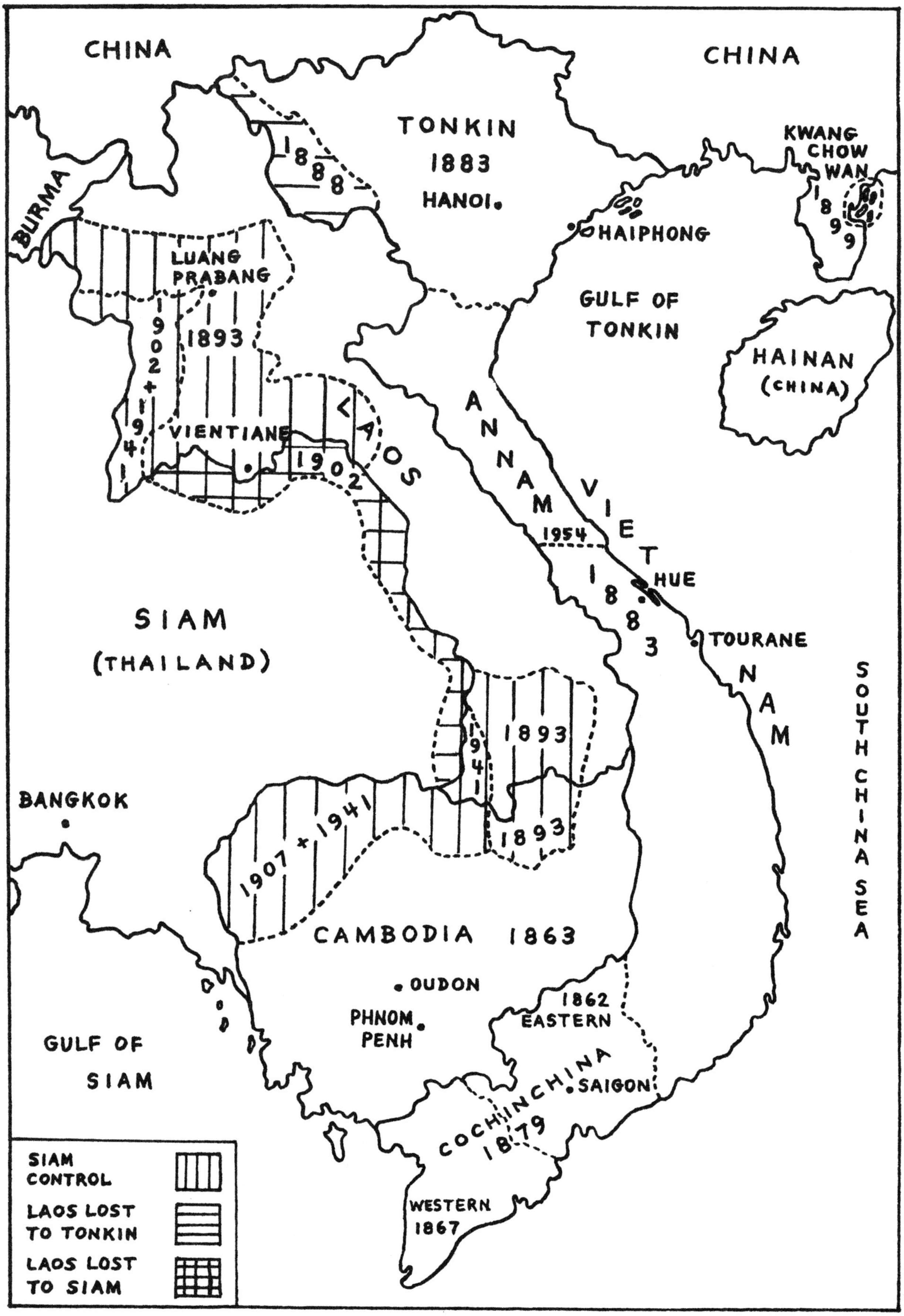

CHINA
CHINA
TONKIN
1883
HANOI
1888
KWANG
CHOW
WAN
1899
BURMA
HAIPHONG
LUANG
PRABANG
1902 + 1941
1893
GULF OF
TONKIN
HAINAN
(CHINA)
LAOS
VIENTIANE
1902
ANNAM
VIET
1954
HUE
1883
SIAM
(THAILAND)
TOURANE
NAM
SOUTH CHINA SEA
1893
1941
1893
BANGKOK
1907 + 1941
1893
CAMBODIA 1863
OUDON
1862
EASTERN
PHNOM
PENH
GULF OF
SIAM
COCHINCHINA
SAIGON
1879
SIAM
CONTROL
LAOS LOST
TO TONKIN
LAOS LOST
TO SIAM
WESTERN
1867

FRENCH INDOCHINA

1885-1951

The French Indochina administration governing the Protectorates of Annam, Cambodia, Tonkin, and the Colony of Cochinchina was created by the decree of 22 December 1885. In 1888 an area northwest of Tonkin in Laos was annexed to the Protectorate of Tonkin because this area had recently paid allegiance to Viet Nam. A Treaty of Protectorate was signed with the King of Luang Prabang in 1893 and the remainder of Laos was added to Indochina. Thailand renounced all claims to Laos and Cambodia after some political and military maneuvering, and the final boundary lines were completed in 1907.

The first circulation strikes of the 1 Piastre(Dollar) coin were introduced in 1885 with the other coins of the Cochinchina series, except the Sapeque, but all now with Indochina on reverse. The Mexican Piastre(8 Reales) was also continued in circulation as legal tender until about 1904. The Sapeque, or 1/5 Cent, with Indochina on the reverse was reintroduced in 1887. The most widely known of the rare coins described in this book is the 1890 1 Piastre with about 10 known out of an issue halted at 6,108 because of the fluctuating price of silver.

In 1891 the Banque de l'Indochine(Bank of Indochina) notes of 5, 20 and 100 Dollars printed by the Bank of France were continued with the decrees of 21 January 1875 and 20 February 1888. The notes are all blue in color with the issuing cities of Saigon or Haiphong handstamped and the issue dates handwritten. Another series of notes was introduced in 1892 with a new 1 Dollar denomination to replace the discontinued 1 Piastre coins. The 1 Dollar note was issued only with the printed 3 August 1891 issue date and in blue for Saigon and Haiphong. The other denominations were also issued in blue except the Haiphong issues were now printed in red. The city names were handstamped but the issue dates were now printed on all notes.

The decree of 8 July 1895 reduced the weight of all Indochina coins except the Sapeque. The 1895 silver coins were issued in both weights and with the same designs as previous years, but there was only the heavier weight 1 Cent with an inscription change on the obverse side of the coin for 1895. The new lower weight 1 Cent was not introduced until 1896 and with a completely changed design and holed. Counterfeits of the 1 Piastre coins have been found in silver-plated lead. The Paris Mint's chief engraver retired in 1896 with his Fasces sign and the new engraver's sign of a Torch was introduced in the same year. The 10 and 20 Cents coins have been discovered with each sign and, with continued searching, the author expects to see all other 1896 denominations with each sign, too. Another series of Bank of Indochina notes was introduced in 1897. The 1 Dollar note was still printed with the 3 August 1891 issue date, but the color was changed to red-brown for Saigon and Haiphong. The other bank note colors continued in blue for Saigon and red for Haiphong. The 1 Dollar note's city names were still handstamped, but the 5, 20 and 100 Dollars notes now had printed city names.

The decree of 14 April 1898 reduced the silver weight of the 10 and 20 Cents coins by lowering the purity from .900 to .835 and increasing the copper weight proportionally. The 16 May 1900 decree was added to a newly printed stock of 5, 20 and 100 dollars notes in 1902. The steady minting of 1 Piastre coins since 1893 and the people's preference for hard currency slowed down the issuing of 1 Dollar notes. Large stocks of these notes with 21 January 1875 and 20 February 1888 decrees were still available for issue, thus eliminating the need to print them. In 1903 the 5 and 100 Dollars note stocks were exhausted and new notes were printed but now with Piastre as the only denomination, dropping the Dollar. In 1907 new 20 Dollars notes were printed with Piastre as the only denomination, but also with the new decree of 3 April 1901.

The Sapeque coin was discontinued in 1902 and completely withdrawn from circulation in 1914. The 1 Cent coin introduced in 1896 was discontinued in 1906 and reintroduced in 1908 with a lower weight and a minor design change. There are several variations of 1906 and 1908 1 Cent coins besides the ones listed in this volume, but all seen or known by the author are trails, patterns or other non-circulation type pieces. The 1 Dollar note stocks from 1897 were finally exhausted and it was reprinted sometime after 1907 with Piastre as the only denomination and the 1875, 1888, 1900 and 1901 decrees. The red-brown color, 3 August 1891 issue date, and the handstamped Saigon and Haiphong city names were continued, while all other notes had their city names printed since the late 1890's. In 1909 the Paris Mint muled many of the 20 Cents coins with the reverse of the coins minted from 1895 to 1897. This is the only known mule in the French Indochina series of coins and notes.

A newly designed series of Bank of Indochina 5, 20 and 100 Piastres notes was introduced in 1913 with the Saigon issues still blue in color but the Haiphong color changed to green.

When World War I erupted, people started hoarding coins with intrinsic value and they quickly disappeared from circulation in Indochina. The administration authorized the Bank of Indochina to issue 10, 20 and 50 Cents notes on 6 October 1919. These notes were the first to be printed outside the Bank of France(BOF) and also the first not to use its numbering system. This BOF system has a block number with a letter prefix(e.g.J.101) and another number(e.g.,999) without prefix. The letter is for each 1,000 notes in a block of 25,000, with A for zero, J for 8,000, X, Y and Z for 21, 22 and 23,000 and W for 24,000. W was chosen as the last letter since it is not used in the French language and I was dropped because it could be confused with the number one. The sample's serial number is derived by subtracting one from the block number, multiplying this number by 25,000, adding 8,000(e.g., J‘8,000) and then adding the number 999 for a total of 2,508,999. The first note is always A.1 000.

Following World War I, the Paris Mint had tremendous domestic and colonial demands for coins and was required to contract with foreign mints for production above its capabilities. The San Francisco Mint struck, with no mintmarks, 1 Cent coins dated 1920 and 1921, 10 and 20 Cents coins dated 1920, and 1 Piastre coins dated 1921 and 1922. The 10 and 20 Cents coins are often found with a grainy appearance. Their reverse designs were modified and the silver content was adjusted to only .400 and .600 copper, while all other coins were of their original designs and metal compositions. The Heaton Mint in Birmingham, England also struck 1 Piastre coins dated 1921 and 1922 but with their H mintmark.

In 1920 5 and 100 Piastres notes were the first to be introduced without any decrees printed on their face sides. The stocks of the 1 and 20 Piastres notes were apparently sufficient and did not require printing at this time. According to known dates and block numbers, it appears that series of complete blocks of 25,000 notes were printed for each day between certain dates except Sundays and holidays. Some days a portion of the block was allocated for Haiphong notes. Looking back to earlier bank note issues it appears that with a few more dates in each variety, all dates of issue can eventually be determined. In 1921 a decree again reduced the purity of the 10 and 20 Cents coins. The composition was changed to .68 silver and .32 copper. This was the last reduction in the purity of these denominations. Following on the heels of the reduction in purity of the 10 and 20 Cents coins, a new series of coins with new denominations for Indochina was started in 1923. The first coin was a holed 5 Cents denomination in copper-nickel with the metal changing in 1938 to nickel-brass and both metal alloys being issued in that year. These very similar 1938 dated coins can be differentiated by their thickness and weight. The nickel-brass coins are about .3 millimeter thinner but a more easily recognizable 1 gram lighter than the copper-nickel coins. Counterfeits of the 5 Cents coins have been found in zinc. There is no decree or official record of the administration ever authorizing their manufacture in this metal.

Several new designs of Bank of Indochina notes were introduced in 1923. The 1, 5 and 100 Piastres were new designs and the first notes issued without city names and issue dates, but the blue 20 Piastres Saigon and green 100 Piastres Haiphong notes, as their issue cities, were continued from the previous series. Another series of notes was introduced in 1927 with a new 20 Piastres design, without city names and issue dates, and the 100 Piastres Haiphong notes were completely discontinued. A 1924 1 Cent with the Thunderbolt mintmark of the Poissy Mint has been reported with a 7,633,171 mintage, but all are believed to have melted at the mint. The 1895 series of 1 Piastre coins was halted in 1928 but the 1923 series was continued in 1931 with a new Piastre coin of a new lighter weight and design. The Paris Mint's chief engraver retired in 1931 with his Torch sign and the new engraver's sign of a Wing was introduced in the same year. The 1931 1 Cent coin has been discovered with each sign and, with continued searching, the author expects to see a 1931 1 Piastre with each sign, too.

Newly designed 1 and 5 Piastres notes were introduced in 1933 with the 100 Piastres design continuing from the previous series. Soon after issue the 5 Piastres notes were counterfeited on authentic watermarked paper. Where or how the counterfeiters acquired this paper is still unknown. The counterfeit notes are excellent copies of the authentic notes except that the block and serial numbers and letters are not perfectly copied. Besides that the counterfeiters did not know the Bank of France system of numbering 25,000 notes within each block number. The Bank of Indochina quickly altered the face of both new notes by changing the 1 in the upper right hand corner from blue to red, and cutting out the design in the 5 Piastres' upper right hand corner and leaving the 5 there in the white margin of the note. A 20 Piastres note in specimen is known in a new and smaller design and with the same signatures as the above notes but none are known to have been printed for circulation. The 20 Piastres notes' history of low popularity which usually had stocks of this denomination carrying over into new series, and the 1936 series of notes appearing in less than three years, leaves little chance that this note was issued for the 1933 series.

The 1923 series of coins was continued with a new holed ½ Cent denomination in 1935 in bronze with the metal changing to zinc in 1939 with both alloys being issued in 1939 and 1940. It appears the Vietnamese stopped manufacturing their own holed coins in about 1935, when the ½ Cent was introduced. In 1936 the Bank of Indochina designs of 1933 were continued with new signatures and with the newly designed 20 Piastres note finally making its appearance. A completely new denomination of 500 Piastres was introduced with this series in 1939. The year 1939 also saw the introduction of newly designed 10 and 20 Cents coins minted in pure nickel and copper-nickel. The nickel 20 Cents coin was the first use of the security edge for Indochina coinage. The different metal coins can be easily identified with a magnet(pure nickel is magnetic), by their edges, and by having or not having small dots left and right of the date. Counterfeits of the 10 and 20 Cents coins have been found in lead.

The clouds of World War II were spreading toward Indochina and as in previous wars, the people started hoarding coins with intrinsic value. The ½, 1 and 5 Cents coins were fast becoming the only coins in circulation. The newly designed 10 and 20 Cents coins were slow in arriving from France and could not completely fill the void of change in circulation when they did arrive, so the administration issued a decree in 1939 authorizing itself to print fractional notes of 10, 20 and 50 Cents. There are several signature varieties of these notes printed by the Imprimerie d'Extreme Orient(IDEO) in Hanoi. The first signature variety has been found with and without the denomination in Lao on the back. After printing, these notes were shipped to the printing firm of Imprimerie C. Ardin & Fil(ICAF) in Saigon for numbering and cutting, and then transferred to the Saigon branch of the Bank of Indochina for issuing. The ICAF was an old established private company that had been designing and printing stocks, bonds, tokens and other papers for many years. The notes have six digit serial numbers followed with a one or two letter suffix. The last variety of the 10 Cents note has a different numbering system with a two letter prefix, three numeric digits, then a period and three more digits. The first numbering system was done at ICAF, but the origin of the second has not been determined. The Paris Mint completed the 1923 series of coins with a redesigned 1 Cent in zinc in 1940 to replace the bronze 1 Cent coins discontinued in 1939. France was converting its domestic and colonial copper alloy coinage to baser metals and utilizing the copper to manufacture war supplies. The Paris Mint could not keep up with the demands for these new coins and the San Francisco Mint was contracted again to mint coins for Indochina. In 1940 the San Francisco Mint struck 25,270,000 nickel 10 Cents and the Paris Mint struck 235,000, all exactly the same with no mintmark.

When Germany defeated France on 16 June 1940, Indochina became isolated from its main source of coins and bank notes. The last shipment of coins must have been the bronze and zinc ½ Cent, zinc 1 Cent, nickel 10 Cents, and a complete series of bank notes. There was now no transport available between France and Indochina, but the lines of communication were still open to the United States before it entered the war. The San Francisco Mint shipped 30,745,000 10 Cents and 25,000,000 20 Cents copper-nickel coins dated 1941 with an S mintmark to Indochina before the Japanese troops entered Saigon on 28 July 1941 and Hanoi on 7 December 1941.

The period from 1942 to 1945 was a very difficult one for the maker of coins and notes in Indochina. The lost contact with France and the United States eliminated most supplies of paper, inks, chemicals, parts, tools and other materials necessary for high quality output. Cannibalization and improvision during this period put a heavy strain on still functioning machines and people, creating many varieties of coins and notes. Paper and some limited ink producing facilities were available but the supplies of chemicals declined rapidly which could produce the quality required for bank notes. Substitutes created many shades of ink and paper. Distinct shades of inks will be listed for each note, but the difficulty in determining the difference between an issued shade of paper, or paper that has toned or yellowed because of climate or age is nearly impossible, which prevents listing them. Coin varieties will be listed but planchet defects or errors will not be listed.

In late 1940 the administration authorized the Ecole Pratique d'Hanoi to fabricate zinc 1 Cent coins using the Paris Mint specimen of 1940 as a model. The 1940 Paris Mint coins have a disc emblem on the Liberty Cap and the 1940 and 1941 Hanoi coins have a Lotus flower in 11 and 12 petal varieties. A decree of 15 October 1942 authorized the creation of 1/4 Cent in zinc and the Osaka Mint in Japan was contracted to mint them. Hundreds of millions of the coins were minted with dates from 1942 to 1944 but only several hundreds of thousands ever reached Indochina because of the lack of ships and the higher priority war materials had over coins. Most of the coins reaching Indochina were dated 1942, a few 1943, but none of the 1944's. The entire remaining stock at Osaka was melted except one of each date for the mint museum and whatever a few employees put in their pockets. There are no zinc 1941 dated 1/4 Cent coins as reported by some sources, but there are lead counterfeits. By 1942 the bronze 1 Cent coins last issued in 1939 were being hoarded and withdrawn from circulation because of the inflated value of copper. Due to manufacturing difficulties or a shortage of metal the zinc 1 Cent coins minted in Hanoi were not meeting the demand for this denomination coin. A decree authorized the Ecole Pratique d'Hanoi to fabricate aluminum 1 and 5 Cents coins dated 1943. No other legal tender coins were authorized or manufactured in Indochina during World War II.

In 1941 the administration authorized the Imprimerie d'Extreme Orient(IDEO) in Hanoi to print newly designed fractional notes of 5, 10, 20 and 50 Cents. The first 5 Cents variety was numbered and cut at the Imprimerie C. Ardin & Fil in Saigon as the 1939 fractional notes, but the second variety 5 Cents and all other denominations are numbered with the system found on the last variety of the 1939 10 Cents notes. Not until 1943 was the supply exhausted of 1, 5, 20, 100 and 500 Piastres notes for the Bank of Indochina that were shipped into Indochina just before the war. The Bank of Indochina then contracted the IDEO to print notes in all of the pre-war denominations, but of new designs. Numerous varieties of colors, numbering, paper, watermarks, etc., are found in this series of notes. The 1 Piastre notes were issued with seven digit serial numbers and a variety with a letter in the first digit. The letter appears to be for each million notes above ten million. The 5 Piastres notes have a one letter prefix followed with six or seven numbers. With six numbers, the letter and first three numbers are the block numbers and letter, as used to compute the serial numbers in the Bank of France(BOF) system, followed by three more numbers for the last three digits of the serial number. The letter for the seven number system appears to be for each five hundred thousand notes. The first variety of the 20 Piastres and the 100 Piastres second and third varieties use the left letter and six numbers, while the other 20 Piastres, the first 100 Piastres, and both 500 Piastres varieties, use the right letter and numbers to compute the serial numbers as in the BOF system.

In some areas of Indochina coins and paper money were not always available in the marketplace in the right denominations to make change at the exact time of the transaction. The people tore their notes in half to make change despite a decree which prohibited this practice. IDEO-printed notes from 5 Cents to 500 Piastres can be found taped together and only in halves. During the last month of the way, the Japanese took complete control of the Bank of Indochina. Many millions of Piastres were issued to their military and civilian organizations. After the war many of the higher denomination notes issued during this period were demonetized. In September 1945 the British occupied the south and the Chinese north of the 16th parallel for the purpose of disarming the Japanese. The British effort allowed the French to regain control almost immediately, but the Chinese favored the Vietnamese independence movement and did not allow the return of the French military forces. The Chinese Army brought Central Bank of China Customs Gold Unit notes with them for use as their occupation currency. These notes will be fully described in a volume about Chinese coins, notes and tokens used in Southeast Asia. There were also Cambodian and Laotian independence movements but the French regained control within a matter of a few months. With the French return aluminum and copper-nickel coins of 5, 10, 20 Cents and

1 Piastre in the 1939 coin design and a copper-nickel 50 Cents in the old silver design were placed in circulation along with 50 and 100 Piastres notes printed in the United States, and 10 and 100 Piastres notes printed in England. The 10 and 50 Piastres notes were the first notes of their denomination to appear in Indochina.

In early 1946, the Bank of Indochina decided to demonetize the 500 Piastres notes printed at IDEO; then the Bank of Indochina issued 1, 5, 20, 100 and 500 Piastres notes printed at the Bank of France. Several of the denominations have a second variety in the different styles of Lao sanskrit characters on the back of the notes. There is also a common uncataloged error in the 1 Piastre second variety with no dot under the letter O in the Vietnamese word of MOT. The 100 Piastres' size and watermark show it to be a note which would have been issued before World War II when the size of the notes was being reduced, but the war interfered with its shipment to Indochina.

In October 1946 the 100 Piastres notes printed in Hanoi were also demonetized. During 1947 the French regained partial control of Viet Nam north of the 16th parallel, after the Chinese departed in the summer of 1946, and some political and military maneuvering with the Vietnamese. During World War II, the Japanese printed 1 and 5 Piastres notes for the Bank of Indochina. The 1 Piastre note was not issued until 1949, but the 5 Piastres was never issued and is known only in specimen or as an unnumbered and unsigned note. The 1 Piastre notes of the 1945 series, and printed in the United States, were not issued until 1951, except letter B notes, which were declared non legal tender after they were stolen in the Philippines enroute to Indochina.

The states of Viet Nam, Cambodia and Laos had been pressuring the French for more independence since the close of World War II. In 1951, each country was allowed to create its own national bank and the privilege of issuing bank notes was transferred from the Bank of Indochina to the Institut d'Emission des Etats du Cambodge, du Laos et du Viet Nam(Issuing Office of the States of Cambodia, Laos and Viet Nam). Bank of Indochina notes were issued through 1953 until sufficient number of the Issuing Office notes for each country were available for issue. The last note of French Indochina in 1951 really belongs to this new organization, but since it was used in all countries like the Bank of Indochina notes, and not like later separate issues for each country, it is cataloged here in French Indochina.

FRENCH INDOCHINA COIN — LEGAL TENDER

SERIES 1885

Government: Colony of Cochinchina and Protectorates of Annam, Cambodia and Tonkin

Governor: Charles Thompson

Minted at: Paris Mint, France

Mint Director: Jean Ruau (Horn)

Designer: Auguste Barre

Engraver: Jean Lagrange (Fasces) and Henri Patey (Torch)

Dates of Issue: 1885 - 1902

cty, code & number	denomination	diameter	thickness	weight	metal	edge	rarity
FI C 1	Sapeque (1/5Cent)	20.0mm	.75mm	2.03grams	Bronze	Smooth	1
FI C 2a	1 Cent	31.0	1.75	10.0	Bronze	Smooth	1
2b		31.0	1.75	10.0	Bronze	Smooth	5
FI C 3a	10 Cents	19.0	1.0	2.721	Silver	Reeded	4
FI C 4a	20 Cents	26.0	1.0	5.443	Silver	Reeded	4
FI C 5a	50 Cents	29.0	2.0	13.607	Silver	Reeded	4
FI C 6a	1 Piastre	39.0	2.5	27.215	Silver	Reeded	2

Metal: Bronze (.85 copper and .15 tin) and Silver (.90 and .10 copper)

Mintmark: A **Mint Director's Sign:** Horn **Engraver's Sign:** Fasces or Torch

Obverse: S: INDO-CHINE FRANCAISE around top edge. Date bottom edge with mintmark above, Mint Director's sign left and Engraver's sign right. 4.5mm square hole center. 1C-1P:REPUBLIQUE FRANCAISE around top edge. Symbolic figure of France seated and holding fasces with anchor behind and grain standing before. 1C: A.B bottom right under France, mintmark bottom center with straight and beaded circles around. Date bottom edge with Mint Director's sign left and Engraver's right. 2b: UN CENTIEME DE PIASTRE around top edge. 10C-1P: Date bottom edge with BARRE left.

Reverse: S: Eight Vietnamese(Chinese-style) characters around square hole meaning (two parts of thousand) one-fifth cent. 1C: INDO-CHINE FRANCAISE around top edge and POIDS 10 GR at bottom edge. Rectangle in horizontal position around four Vietnamese (Chinese-style) characters meaning (one part of hundred) one cent. 1 to left and C right of rectangle with beaded circle around all. 10C-1P: INDO-CHINE FRANCAISE around top edge and wreath of leaves and berries around center area tied with a ribbon at the base. At top of base is mintmark with Mint Director's sign left and Engravers's right, and denomination in two lines center except 1 Piastre has PIASTRE DE COMMERCE in three lines. 10C: TITRE 0.900. POIDS 2.721, 20C: 5.433, 50C: 13,607 GR., and 1P: 27, 215 GR. around bottom edge.

FRENCH INDOCHINA COIN — LEGAL TENDER

SERIES 1885

FI C 1

FI C 3a

FI C 2a

FI C 2b

FI C 4a

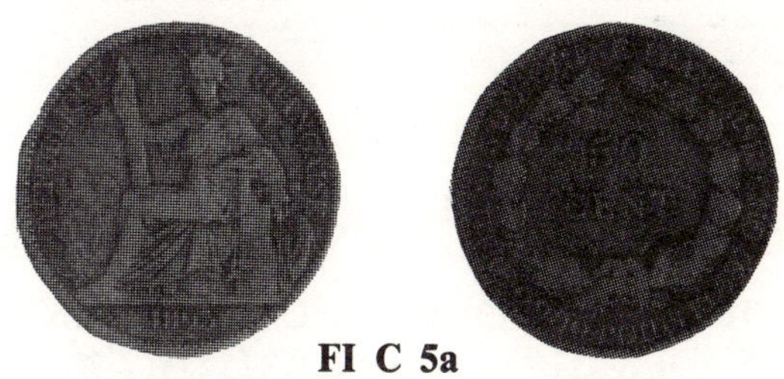

FI C 5a

FI C 6a

FRENCH INDOCHINA NOTE — LEGAL TENDER

SERIES 1888 A

Government: Colony of Cochinchina and Protectorates of Annam, Cambodia and Tonkin

Governor: Jean de Lanessan

Printed at: Bank of France, Paris, France

Designer: A. Bramtot and Georges Duval

Engraver: Ch. Wullschleger and J. Robert

Dates of Issue: 1891 - 1892

cty, code & number	denomination	width	length	major color	signatures	rarity
FI N 1a	5 Dollars	94mm	181mm	Blue	1 and 2	9
1b		94	181	Blue	1 and 2	9
FI N 2a	20 Dollars	118	207	Blue	1 and 2	9
2b		118	207	Blue	1 and 2	9
FI N 3a	100 Dollars	145	215	Blue	1 and 2	9
3b		145	215	Blue	1 and 2	9

Paper: Thin White

Watermark: Head of Mercury

Face: 5-100D: BANQUE DE L'INDOCHINE in one line at top center or top right(20D) center with DECRETS DES 21 JANVIER 1875 ET 20 FEVRIER 1888 above and handstamped SAIGON(a) or HAIPHONG(b) with handwritten date below. A-BRAMTOT ET G.DUVAL.FEC. in lower left and CH-WULLSCHLEGER.SC. or J.ROBERT SC.(100D) in lower right margins. 5D: FIVE DOLLARS center and CINQ PIASTRES right. Watermark circle upper left and seated Neptune left. 20D: TWENTY DOLLARS left center and VINGT PIASTRES right. Elephants standing in front of columns left and right. Stand with potted plant atop at bottom center, French woman and cow left, Indian woman and tiger right. Watermark area center. 100D: ONE HUNDRED DOLLARS left and CENT PIASTRES right. Vasco de Gama standing in front of column left and Oriental male right. Ships and boats bottom center.

Back: 5-100D: Various designs with open areas for Vietnamese(Chinese-style) characters describing the notes as issues of the Bank of Indochina in the colony of Cochinchina, their denomination and that they are payable in silver, and the counterfeiting Article 139 in French.

FRENCH INDOCHINA NOTE — LEGAL TENDER

SERIES 1888 A

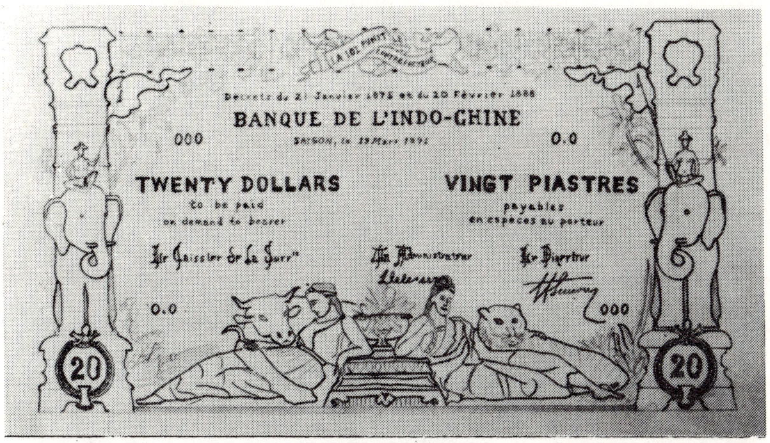

FI N 2a

Author's conception and drawing of 20 Dollars note

FRENCH INDOCHINA NOTE — LEGAL TENDER

SERIES 1888 B

Government: Colony of Cochinchina and Protectorates of Annam, Cambodia and Tonkin

Governor: Jean de Lanessan

Printed at: Bank of France, Paris, France

Designer: A. Bramtot, Georges Duval and Daniel Dupuis

Engraver: Ch. Wullschleger, J. Robert and A. Leveille

Dates of Issue: 1892 - 1899

cty, code & number	denomination	width	length	major color	signatures	rarity
FI N 4a	1 Dollar	105mm	140mm	Blue	1 and 2	7
4b		105	140	Blue	1 and 2	9
FI N 1c	5 Dollars	94	181	Blue	1 and 2	9
1d		94	181	Red	1 and 2	9
FI N 2c	20 Dollars	118	207	Blue	1 and 2	9
2d		118	207	Red	1 and 2	9
FI N 3c	100 Dollars	145	215	Blue	1 and 2	8
3d		145	215	Red	1 and 2	9

Paper: Thin White

Watermark: $1 or Head of Mercury

Face: 1-100D: BANQUE DE L'INDOCHINE in one line top center or top right(20D) center with DECRETS DES 21 JANVIER 1875 ET 20 FEVRIER 1888 above or below(1D) and SAIGON(a and c) or HAIPHONG(b and d) handstamped below, or upper left(1D), with printed date. 1D: ONE DOLLAR center and UNE PIASTRE right. Symbolic figure of France and Oriental woman below left and watermark lower right. DANIEL DUPUIS ET GEORGES DUVAL.FEC. in lower left and A LEVEILLE SC in lower right margins. 5-100D: A-BRAMTOT ET G.DUVAL.FEC. in lower left and CH-WULLSCHLEGER.SC. or J.ROBERT SC.(100D) in lower right margins. 5D: FIVE DOLLARS center and CINQ PIASTRES right. Watermark circle upper left and seated Neptune left. 20D: TWENTY DOLLARS left center and VINGT PIASTRES right. Elephants standing in front of columns left and right. Stand with potted plant atop at bottom center, French woman and cow left, Indian woman and tiger right. Watermark area center. 100D: ONE HUNDRED DOLLARS left and CENT PIASTRES right. Vasco de Gama standing in front of column left and Oriental male right. Ships and boats bottom center.

Back: 1-100D: Various designs with open areas for Vietnamese(Chinese-style) characters describing the notes as issues of the Bank of Indochina, their denomination and that they are payable in silver, and the counterfeiting Article 139 in French.

FRENCH INDOCHINA NOTE — LEGAL TENDER

SERIES 1888 B

FI N 4a

FI N 3c

1 Dollar note courtesy of Roger Outing and the 100 Dollars note from Desire Lacroix's *Numismatique Annamite* courtesy of the American Numismatic Society Library.

FRENCH INDOCHINA COIN — LEGAL TENDER

SERIES 1895

Government:	Colony of Cochinchina and Protectorates of Annam, Cambodia, Laos and Tonkin	**Governor:**	Paul Rousseau
Minted at:	Paris(A) Mint, France, Heaton(H) Mint, Birmingham, England, and San Francisco(None) Mint, California		
Designer:	Auguste Barre and Daniel Dupuis	**Engraver:**	Jean Lagrange (Fasces) and Henri Patey (Torch)

Dates of Issue: 1895 - 1936

cty, code & number	denomination	diameter	thickness	weight	metal	edge	rarity
FI C 7a	1 Cent	27.5mm	1.75mm	7.5grams	Bronze	Smooth	2
FI C 3b	10 Cents	19.0	1.0	2.7	Silver	Reeded	4
FI C 4b	20 Cents	26.0	1.0	5.4	Silver	Reeded	7
FI C 5b	50 Cents	29.0	2.0	13.5	Silver	Reeded	1
FI C 6b	1 Piastre	39.0	2.5	27.0	Silver	Reeded	1

Metal: Bronze (.85 copper and .15 tin), Silver (.90 and .10 copper)

Mintmark: A, H or None **Mint Director's Sign:** Horn **Engraver's Sign:** Fasces or Torch

Obverse: 1C-1P: REPUBLIQUE FRANCAISE along left and right edge. 1C: Mintmark at bottom edge with Mint Director's sign left and Engraver's right. Symbolic figure of France and Indochinese around 4.5mm hole center with 1 CENT in two lines below. DANIEL DUPUIS in very small letters at bottom right edge. 10C-1P: Symbolic figure of France seated holding fasces, anchor behind and grain standing before. Date bottom edge with BARRE left.

Reverse: 1C: INDO-CHINE FRANCAISE along top edge and date at bottom edge. Four Vietnamese (Chinese-style) characters around hole center with beaded circle around. 10C-1P: INDO-CHINE FRANCAISE around top edge and wreath of leaves and berries around center area tied with a ribbon at the base. At top of base is the mintmark or blank with Mint Director's sign left and Engraver's right and denomination in two lines center except 1 Piastre has PIASTRE DE COMMERCE. 10C: TITRE 0,900. POIDS 2GR.7, 20C: 5gr.4, 50D: 13GR.5, and 1P: 27GR. around bottom edge.

FRENCH INDOCHINA COIN — LEGAL TENDER
SERIES 1895

FI C 7a

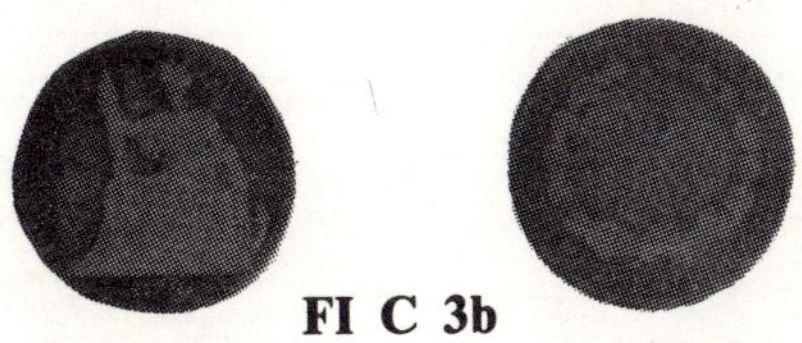

FI C 3b

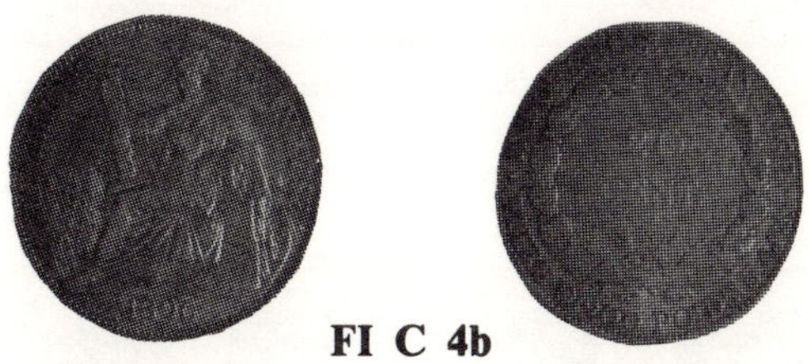

FI C 4b

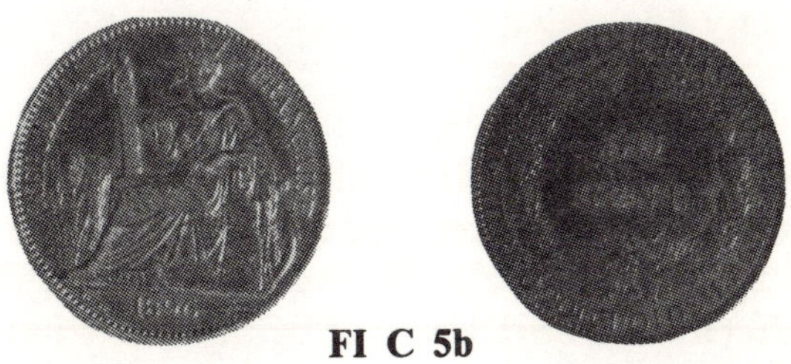

FI C 5b

FI C 6b

FRENCH INDOCHINA NOTE — LEGAL TENDER

SERIES 1888 C

Government: Colony of Cochinchina and Protectorates of Annam, Cambodia, Laos and Tonkin

Governor: Paul Doumer

Printed at: Bank of France, Paris, France

Designer: A. Bramtot, Georges Duval and Daniel Dupuis

Engraver: Ch. Wullschleger, J. Robert and A. Leveille

Dates of Issue: 1897 - 1907

cty, code & number	denomination	width	length	major color	signatures	rarity
FI N 4c	1 Dollar	105mm	140mm	Brown	3 and 2	6
4d		105	140	Brown	3 and 2	7
FI N 1e	5 Dollars	94	181	Blue	1 and 2	8
1f		94	181	Red	1 and 2	9
FI N 2e	20 Dollars	118	207	Blue	1 and 2	9
2f		118	207	Red	1 and 2	9
FI N 3e	100 Dollars	145	215	Blue	1 and 2	9
3f		145	215	Red	1 and 2	9

Paper: Thin White

Watermark: $1 or Head of Mercury

Face: 1-100D: BANQUE DE L'INDOCHINE in one line top center or top right(20D); center with DECRETS DES 21 JANVIER 1875 ET 20 FEVRIER 1888 above or below(1D) and SAIGON(c and e) or HAIPHONG(d and f) printed below, or handstamped upper left(1D), with printed date. 1D: ONE DOLLAR center and UNE PIASTRE right. Symbolic figure of France and Oriental woman below left and watermark lower right. DANIEL DUPUIS ET GEORGES DUVAL.FEC. in lower left and A LEVEILLE SC in lower right margins. 5-100D: A-BRAMTOT ET G.DUVAL.FEC. in lower left and CH-WULLSCHLEGER.SC. or J.ROBERT sc.(100D) in lower right margins. 5D: FIVE DOLLARS center and CINQ PIASTRES right. Watermark circle upper left and seated Neptune left. 20D: TWENTY DOLLARS left center and VINGT PIASTRES right. Elephants standing in front of columns left and right. Stand with potted plant atop at bottom center, French woman and cow left, Indian woman and tiger right. Watermark area center. 100D: ONE HUNDRED DOLLARS left and CENT PIASTRES right. Vasco de Gama standing in front of column left and Oriental male right. Ships and boats bottom center.

Back: 1-100D: Various designs with open areas for Vietnamese(Chinese-style) characters describing the notes as issues of the Bank of Indochina, their denomination and that they are payable in silver, and the counterfeiting Article 139 in French.

FRENCH INDOCHINA NOTE — LEGAL TENDER

SERIES 1888 C

FI N 4d

1 Piastre note courtesy of Roger Outing.

FRENCH INDOCHINA COIN - LEGAL TENDER

SERIES 1898

Government: Colony of Cochinchina and Protectorates of Annam, Cambodia, Laos and Tonkin

Governor: Paul Doumer

Minted at: Paris Mint, France

Designer: Auguste Barre

Engraver: Henri Patey

Dates of Issue: 1898 - 1919

cty, code & number	denomination	diameter	thickness	weight	metal	edge	rarity
FI C 3c	10 Cents	19.0mm	1.0mm	2.7grams	Silver	Reeded	1
FI C 4c	20 Cents	26.0	1.0	5.4	Silver	Reeded	2
(Mule)		26.0	1.0	5.4	Silver	Reeded	3

Metal: Silver (.835 and .165 copper)

Mintmark: A **Mint Director's Sign:** Horn **Engraver's Sign:** Torch

Obverse: REPUBLIQUE FRANCAISE around top edge. Symbolic figure of France seated holding fasces, anchor behind and grain standing before. Date bottom edge with BARRE left.

Reverse: INDO-CHINE FRANCAISE around top edge and wreath of leaves and berries around center area tied with a ribbon at the base. At top of base is mintmark with Mint Director's sign left and Engraver's right, and denomination in two lines center. 10C: TITRE 0,835. POIDS 2GR.7 and 20C: 5GR.4 around bottom edge. 20C(Mule): TITRE 0,900. POIDS 5GR.4.

FRENCH INDOCHINA COIN — LEGAL TENDER

SERIES 1898

FI C 3c

FI C 4c

FRENCH INDOCHINA NOTE — LEGAL TENDER

SERIES 1900 A

Government: Colony of Cochinchina and Protectorates of Annam, Cambodia, Laos and Tonkin

Governor: Paul Beau

Printed at: Bank of France, Paris, France

Designer: A. Bramtot and Georges Duval

Engraver: Ch. Wullschleger and J. Robert

Dates of Issue: 1902 - 1905

cty, code & number	denomination	width	length	major color	signatures	rarity
FI N 1g	5 Dollars	94mm	181mm	Blue	4 and 2	9
1h		94	181	Red	4 and 2	9
FI N 2g	20 Dollars	118	207	Blue	4 and 2	8
2h		118	207	Red	4 and 2	9
FI N 3g	100 Dollars	145	215	Blue	4 and 2	8
3h		145	215	Red	4 and 2	9

Paper: Thin White

Watermark: Head of Mercury

Face: 5-100D: BANQUE DE L'INDOCHINE in one line top center or top right(20D) center with DECRETS DES 21 JANVIER 1875, 20 FEVRIER 1888 ET 16 MAI 1900 above and SAIGON(g) or HAIPHONG(h) and date below. A-BRAMTOT ET G.DUVAL.FEC. in lower left and CH.WULLSCHLEGER.SC. or J.ROBERT SC.(100D) in lower right margins. 5D: FIVE DOLLARS center and CINQ PIASTRES right. Watermark circle upper left and seated Neptune left. 20D: TWENTY DOLLARS left center and VINGT PIASTRES right. Elephants standing in front of columns left and right. Stand with potted plant atop at bottom center, French woman and cow left, Indian woman and tiger right. Watermark area center. 100D: ONE HUNDRED DOLLARS left and CENT PIASTRES right. Vasco de Gama standing in front of column left and Oriental male right. Ships and boats bottom center.

Back: 5-100D: Various designs with open areas for Vietnamese(Chinese-style) characters describing the notes as issues of the Bank of Indochina, their denomination and that they are payable in silver, and the counterfeiting Article 139 in French.

FRENCH INDOCHINA NOTE — LEGAL TENDER

SERIES 1900 A

FI N 3g

100 Dollars note courtesy of Roger Outing.

FRENCH INDOCHINA NOTE — LEGAL TENDER

SERIES 1900 B

Government:	Colony of Cochinchina and Protectorates	**Governor:**	Paul Beau
Printed at:	Bank of France, Paris, France		
Designer:	A. Bramtot and Georges Duval	**Engraver:**	Ch. Wullschleger and J. Robert

Dates of Issue: 1903 - 1914

cty, code & number	denomination	width	length	major color	signatures	rarity
FI N 1i	5 Piastres	94mm	181mm	Blue	4 and 2	9
1j		94	181	Red	4 and 2	9
FI N 3i	100 Piastres	145	215	Blue	4 and 2	6
3j		145	215	Red	4 and 2	7

Paper: Thin White

Watermark: Head of Mercury

Face: 5 and 100P: BANQUE DE L'INDOCHINE in one line top center with DECRETS DES 21 JANVIER 1875, 20 FEVRIER 1888 ET 16 MAI 1900 above and SAIGON(i) or HAIPHONG(j) and date below. A-BRAMTOT ET G. DUVAL.FEC. in lower left and CH-WULLSCHLEGER.SC. or J.ROBERT SC.(100P) in lower right margins. 5P: CINQ PIASTRES center and right. Watermark circle upper left and seated Neptune left. 100P: CENT PIASTRES left and right. Vasco de Gama standing in front of column left and Oriental male right. Ships and boats bottom center.

Back: 5 and 100P: Various designs with open areas for Vietnamese(Chinese-style) characters describing the notes as issues of the Bank of Indochina, their denomination and that they are payable in silver, and the counterfeiting Article 139 in French.

FRENCH INDOCHINA NOTE — LEGAL TENDER

SERIES 1900 B

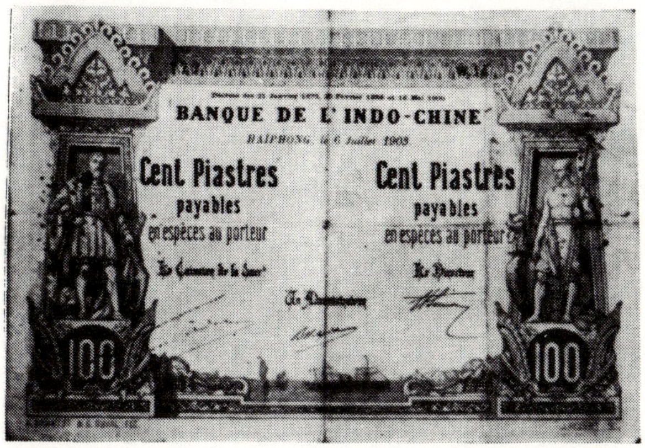

FI N 3i

100 Piastres note courtesy of Roger Outing.

FRENCH INDOCHINA NOTE — LEGAL TENDER
SERIES 1901 A

Government: Colony of Cochinchina and Protectorates of Annam, Cambodia, Laos and Tonkin

Governor: Paul Beau

Printed At: Bank of France, Paris, France

Designer: A. Bramtot and Georges Duval

Engraver: Ch. Wullschleger

Dates of Issue: 1907 — 1917

cty, code & number	denomination	width	length	major color	signatures	rarity
FI N 2i	20 Piastres	118mm	207mm	Blue	4 and 2	9
2j		118	207	Red	4 and 2	8

Paper: Thin White

Watermark: Head of Mercury

Face: BANQUE DE L'INDOCHINE in one line top center with DECRETS DES 21 JANVIER 1875, 20 FEVRIER 1888, 16 MAI 1900 and 3 AVRIL 1901 below, and SAIGON(i) or HAIPHONG(j) and date below the above lines. VINGT PIASTRES left center and right. Stand with potted plant atop at bottom center, French woman and cow left, Indian woman and tiger right. A-BRAMTOT ET G.DUVAL.FEC. in lower left and CH-WULLSCHLEGER.SC. in lower right margin.

Back: Geometric design with open areas for Vietnamese(Chinese-style) characters describing the notes as issues of the Bank of Indochina, their denomination and that they are payable in silver, and the counterfeiting Article 139 in French.

FRENCH INDOCHINA NOTE — LEGAL TENDER

SERIES 1901 A

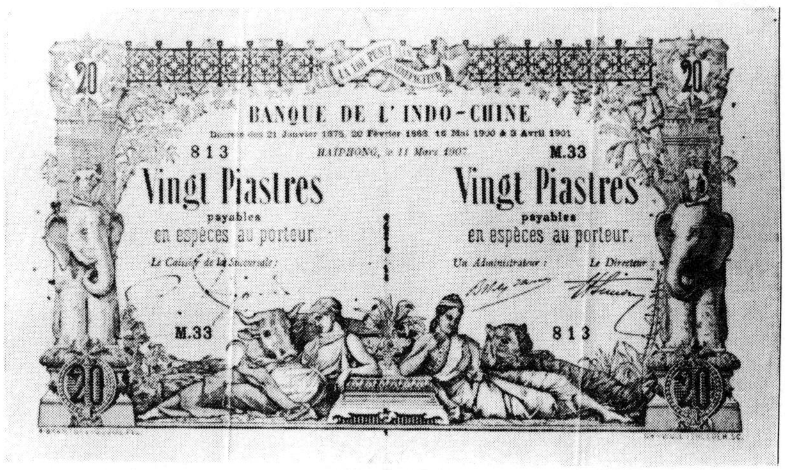

FI N 2j

20 Piastres note courtesy of Dr. Melvin P. Hennisch.

FRENCH INDOCHINA COIN — LEGAL TENDER

SERIES 1908

Government: Colony of Cochinchina and Protectorates of Annam, Cambodia, Laos and Tonkin

Governor: Gabriel Bonhoure

Minted at: Paris(A) and Poissy(TB) Mints, France and San Francisco(None) Mint, California

Designer: Daniel Dupuis

Engraver: Henri Patey (Torch) and Lucien Bazor (Wing)

Dates of Issue: 1908 - 1939

cty, code & number	denomination	diameter	thickness	weight	metal	edge	rarity
FI C 7b	1 Cent	26.0mm	1.4mm	7.0grams	Bronze	Smooth	1

Metal: Bronze (.85 copper and .15 tin)

Mintmark: A, Thunderbolt(Tb) or None

Mint Director's Sign: Horn or None

Engraver's Sign: Torch, Wing or None

Obverse: REPUBLIQUE FRANCAISE along left and right edge. Mintmark or blank at bottom edge with Mint Director's sign left and Engraver's right. Symbolic figure of France and Indochinese around 4.5mm hole center with 1 CENT in two lines below. DANIEL DUPUIS in very small letters at bottom edge.

Reverse: INDO-CHINE FRANCAISE around top edge with date at bottom. Four Vietnamese (Chinese-style) characters at left, right, top and bottom of center hole meaning (one part of hundred) one cent with beaded circle around.

FRENCH INDOCHINA COIN — LEGAL TENDER
SERIES 1908

FI C 7b

FRENCH INDOCHINA NOTE — LEGAL TENDER
SERIES 1901 B

Government: Colony of Cochinchina and Protectorates of Annam, Cambodia, Laos and Tonkin

Governor: Albert Sarraut

Printed at: Bank of France, Paris, France

Designer: Daniel Dupuis, Georges Duval and H. Bellery Desfontaines

Engraver: A. Leveille, Leon Ruffe and E. Gaspe

Dates of Issue: 1913 - 1923(1P from 1907)

cty, code & number	denomination	width	length	major color	signatures	rarity
FI N 4e	1 Piastre	105mm	140mm	Brown	4 and 2	4
4f		105	140	Brown	4 and 2	5
FI N 5a	5 Piastres	94	181	Blue	4 and 2	4
5b		94	181	Green	4 and 2	5
FI N 6a	20 Piastres	118	207	Blue	4 and 2	5
6b		118	207	Green	4 and 2	6
FI N 7a	100 Piastres	145	215	Blue	4 and 2	5
7b		145	215	Green	4 and 2	6

Paper: Thin White

Watermark: $1 and Head of Vietnamese man

Face: 1-100P: BANQUE DE L'INDOCHINE in one line top center with DECRETS DES 21 JANVIER 1875, 20 FEVRIER 1888, 16 MAI 1900 ET or & (1P) 3 AVRIL 1901 below, printed SAIGON(e and a) or HAIPHONG(f and b) below, or handstamped upper left(1P), with date. 1P: UNE PIASTRE center and right. Symbolic figure of France and Oriental woman seated below left and watermark lower right. DANIEL DUPUIS ET GEORGES DUVAL FEC. in lower left and A LEVEILLE SC in lower right margins. 5P: CINQ PIASTRES across center. Ships and boats lower left and watermark circle lower right, GEORGES DUVAL FEC. in lower left and L RUFFE SC in lower right margins. 20P: VINGT PIASTRES across center. Symbolic figure of France seated left holding sword and two Orientals right. Watermark area lower left. LEON RUFFE SC in lower left and GEORGES DUVAL FECIT in lower right margins. 100P: CENT PIASTRES across center. Vietnamese male right with symbolic figure of France standing behind. Stone lion up on hind legs upper left and watermark area lower left. H. BELLERY DESFONTAINES DEL. in lower left and L RUFFE SC. in lower right margins.

Back: 1-100P: Various designs with open areas for Vietnamese(Chinese-style) characters describing the notes as issues of the Bank of Indochina, their denomination and that they are payable in silver, and the counterfeiting Article 139 in French.

FRENCH INDOCHINA NOTE — LEGAL TENDER

SERIES 1901 B

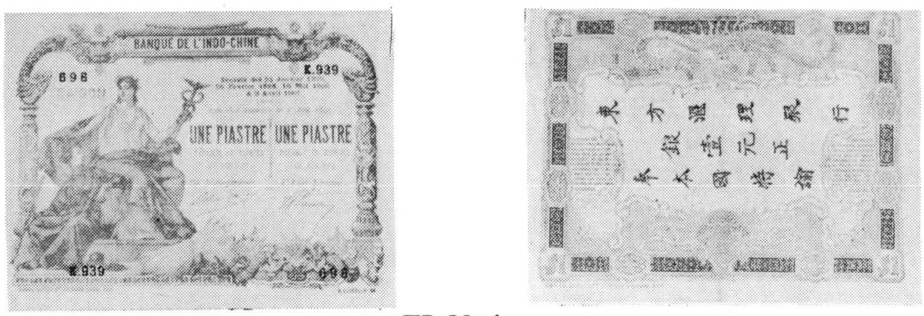

FI N 4e

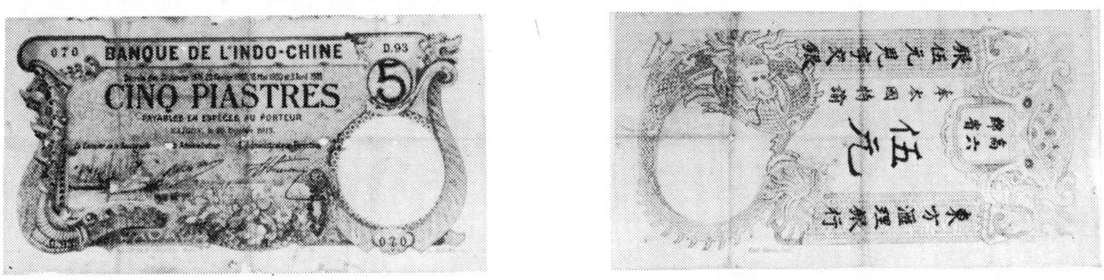

FI N 5a

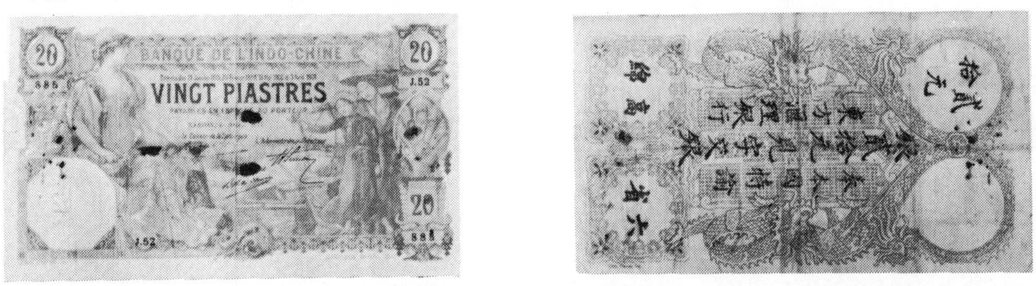

FI N 6a

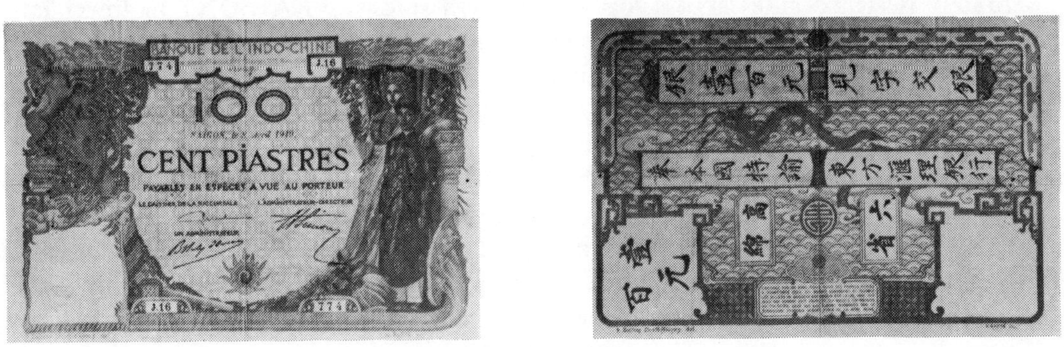

FI N 7a

100 Piastres note courtesy of Clyde M. Reedy.

FRENCH INDOCHINA NOTE — LEGAL TENDER

SERIES 1901 C

Government: Colony of Cochinchina and Protectorates of Annam, Cambodia, Laos and Tonkin **Governor:** Albert Sarraut

Printed at: Chaix, Paris, France

Designer: G. Fraipont **Engraver:** Unknown

Dates of Issue: 1919 - 1921

cty, code & number	denomination	width	length	major color	signatures	rarity
FI N 8a	10 Cents	57mm	84mm	Blue	4 and 2	4
8b		57	84	Blue	5 and 6	5
FI N 9a	20 Cents	61	88	Violet	4 and 2	4
9b		61	88	Violet	4 and 2	5
FI N 10a	50 Cents	67	100	Red	4 and 2	5
10b		67	100	Red	5 and 6	6

Paper: Thin White

Watermark: Wreath around BIC with BFR below.

Face: 10-50C: BANQUE DE L'INDOCHINE in one, or two(20C) lines at top center. Denomination across center with black or red(10b) serial numbers below, and above(50C), or red(8b) block and serial numbers above and below. Elaborately designed gates across top and at each side. G.FRAIPONT at lower left margin or edge(50C). 10C: Two dragons across top center facing center. 20C: Stylized lotus at upper right and left. 50C: Monuments at each side topped with Cambodian-style crowns.

Back: 10-50C: DECRET DU 3 AVRIL 1901 in one line with EMISSION AUTORISEE LE 6 OCTOBRE 1919 in one line below at top of center area with counterfeiting Article 139 in French in bottom. G.FRAIPONT at lower left margin(50C) or edge with and without(9b) in lower right margin. 10C: Elaborate flower design around center area with denomination at lower left and right corners. (8b): Two Chinese characters and Vietnamese GIAY BAC MOT CAT overprinted in center area in red describing the note as a one dime bank note. 20C: Cambodian-style gate across top and at each side with Nagas at top left, middle and right of gate design. 50C: Dragons facing BIC at top center curling down on each side of center area; 50 at all four corners.

FRENCH INDOCHINA NOTE — LEGAL TENDER

SERIES 1901 C

FI N 8b

FI N 9a

FI N 10a

20 Cents note courtesy of Clyde M. Reedy and
50 Cents note courtesy of Pick-Bayerische Hypotheken und Wechsel Bank.

FRENCH INDOCHINA COIN — LEGAL TENDER

SERIES 1920

Government: Colony of Cochinchina and Protectorates of Annam, Cambodia, Laos and Tonkin **Governor:** Maurice Long

Minted at: San Francisco Mint, California

Designer: Auguste Barre **Engraver:** Henri Patey

Dates of Issue: 1920 - 1921

cty, code & number	denomination	diameter	thickness	weight	metal	edge	rarity
FI C 3d	10 Cents	19.0mm	1.0mm	2.7grams	Billion	Reeded	4
FI C 4d	20 Cents	26.0	1.0	5.4	Billion	Reeded	4

Metal: Billion (.600 Copper and .400 Silver)

Mintmark: None **Mint Director's Sign:** None **Engraver's Sign:** None

Obverse: REPUBLIQUE FRANCAISE around top edge. Symbolic figure of France seated holding fasces with anchor behind and grain standing before. Date at bottom edge with BARRE left.

Reverse: INDO-CHINE around top edge and FRANCAISE around bottom edge. Wreath of leaves and berries around center area tied with a ribbon at the base. Denomination in two lines in center.

FRENCH INDOCHINA COIN — LEGAL TENDER

SERIES 1920

FI C 3d

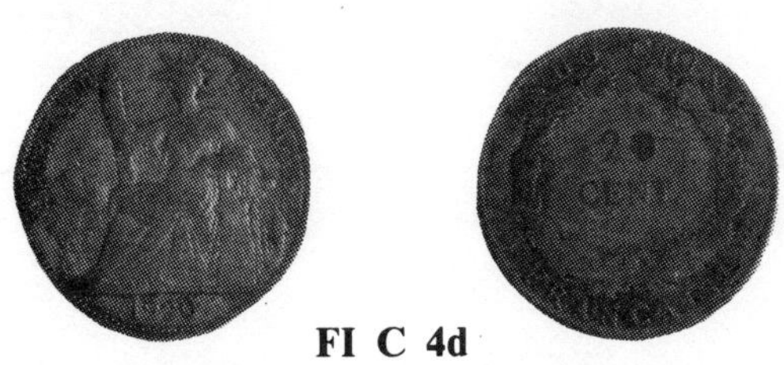

FI C 4d

FRENCH INDOCHINA NOTE — LEGAL TENDER

SERIES 1920

Government:	Colony of Cochinchina and Protectorates of Annam, Cambodia, Laos and Tonkin	**Governor:**	Maurice Long
Printed at:	Bank of France, Paris, France		
Designer:	Georges Duval and H. Bellery Desfontaines	**Engraver:**	Leon Ruffe and E. Gaspe
Dates of Issue:	1920 - 1923		

cty, code & number	denomination	width	length	major color	signatures	rarity
FI N 5c	5 Piastres	94mm	181mm	Blue	4 and 2	4
5d		94	181	Green	4 and 2	5
FI N 7c	100 Piastres	145	215	Blue	4 and 2	5
7d		145	215	Green	4 and 2	8

Paper: Thin White

Watermark: Head of Vietnamese man

Face: 5 and 100P: BANQUE DE L'INDOCHINE top center in one line. L.RUFFE SC. in lower left margin. 5P: CINQ PIASTRES across center with SAIGON(c) or HAIPHONG(d) city names and date printed below. Ships and boats lower left and watermark circle lower right. GEORGES DUVAL FEC. in lower left and L RUFFE SC. in lower right margins. 100P: CENT PIASTRES across center with SAIGON(c) or HAIPHONG(d) city names and date printed below. Vietnamese male right with symbolic figure of France standing behind. Stone lion up on hind legs upper left and watermark area lower left. H.BELLERY DESFONTAINES DEL. in lower left and L RUFFE SC. in lower right margins.

Back: 5 and 100P: Open areas with Vietnamese(Chinese-style) characters describing the notes as issues of the Bank of Indochina, their denomination and that they are payable in silver, and the counterfeiting Article 139 in French. 5P: Dragon's body curled around watermark area left and large dragon head at right. GEO.DUVAL.FEC. in lower left margin. 100P: Dragon center flying through clouds and watermark area lower right. H.BELLERY DESFONTAINES DEL. in lower left and E.GASPE SC. in lower right margins.

FRENCH INDOCHINA NOTE — LEGAL TENDER
SERIES 1920

FI N 5c

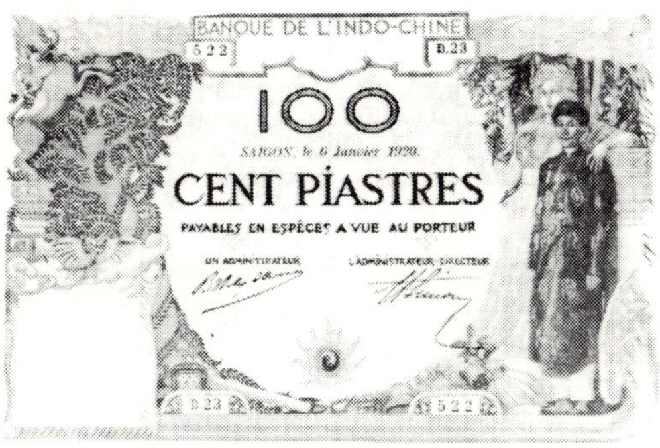

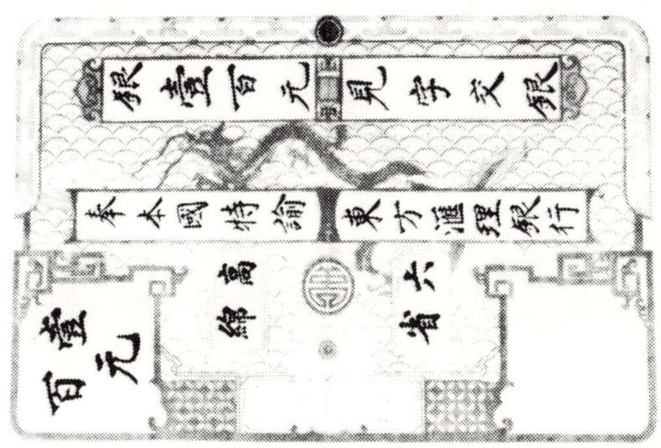

FI N 7c

FRENCH INDOCHINA COIN — LEGAL TENDER

SERIES 1921

Government: Colony of Cochinchina and Protectorates of Annam, Cambodia, Laos and Tonkin

Governor: Maurice Long

Minted at: Paris Mint, France

Designer: Auguste Barre

Engraver: Henri Patey (Torch) and Lucien Bazor (Wing)

Dates of Issue: 1921 - 1937

cty, code & number	denomination	diameter	thickness	weight	metal	edge	rarity
FI C 3e	10 Cents	19.0mm	1.0mm	2.7grams	Silver	Reeded	1
FI C 4e	20 Cents	26.0	1.0	5.4	Silver	Reeded	1

Metal: Silver (.68 and .32 copper)

Mintmark: A or None **Mint Director's Sign:** Horn **Engraver's Sign:** Torch or Wing

Obverse: REPUBLIQUE FRANCAISE around top edge. Symbolic figure of France seated holding fasces with anchor behind and grain standing before. Date bottom edge with BARRE left.

Reverse: INDO-CHINE FRANCAISE around top edge. Wreath of leaves and berries around center area tied with a ribbon at the base. The mintmark (or absence of one) is at top of base with Mint Director's sign left and Engraver's right. Denomination in two lines at center and TITRE 0,680 POIDS 2GR.7(10C) or 5GR.4(20C) around bottom edge.

FRENCH INDOCHINA COIN — LEGAL TENDER

SERIES 1921

FI C 3e

FI C 4e

FRENCH INDOCHINA COIN — LEGAL TENDER

SERIES 1923

Government:	Colony of Cochinchina and Protectorates of Annam, Cambodia, Laos and Tonkin	**Governor:**	Martial Merlin
Minted at:	Paris Mint, France and Ecole Pratique d'Hanoi (9b & c), Tonkin		
Designer:	Em. Lindauer and Henri Patey	**Engraver:**	Henri Patey (Torch) and Lucien Bazor (Wing)
Dates of Issue:	1923 - 1941		

cty, code & number	denomination	diameter	thickness	weight	metal	edge	rarity
FI C 8a	½ Cent	21.0mm	2.0mm	3.7grams	Bronze	Smooth	1
8b		21.0	2.0	3.0	Zinc	Smooth	6
FI C 9a	1 Cent	28.0	1.5	6.0	Zinc	Smooth	5
9b		28.0	1.5	6.0	Zinc	Smooth	1
9c		28.0	1.5	6.0	Zinc	Smooth	5
FI C 10a	5 Cents	24.0	1.7	5.0	Cop-Nic	Smooth	2
10b		24.0	1.4	4.0	Nic-Brass	Smooth	1
FI C 11	1 Piastre	35.0	2.5	20.0	Silver	Reeded	1

Metal: Bronze (.85 copper and .15 tin), Zinc (1.00), Copper-Nickel (.75 and .25), Nickel-Brass (.75 and .25), Silver (.68 and .32 copper)

Mintmark: None **Mint Director's Sign:** Horn or None **Engraver's Sign:** Torch, Wing or None

Obverse: ½C: Liberty Cap with disc emblem at top, wreath of leaves and berries around edge to cap, and large R left and F right of 5mm hole at center. ½C and 1P: EM. LINDAUER at bottom right edge. 1C-1P: REPUBLIQUE FRANCAISE along left and right edge. 1C: Liberty Cap with disc emblem at top. Branch of leaves and berries from bottom to left and right of 5.5mm hole center. 1 CENT in one line at bottom. 9b: 11 petal lotus on cap replacing disc. 9c: 12 petal lotus. 5C: Symbolic head of France with laurel around head at top, cornucopius horns from bottom to left and right of 5.5mm hole. LIBERTE, EGALITE and FRATERNITE on curling ribbon across base of horns and A.PATEY at bottom edge. 1P: Symbolic head of France with laurel around head center.

Reverse: ½-5C: Sheaf of grain from bottom to left and right of hole and date at bottom edge. ½C: INDOCHINE FRANCAISE in two lines at top edge, ½ left and CENT right of hole. ½&5C: Mint Director's sign left and Engraver's right of date. 1C-1P: INDOCHINE FRANCAISE along left and right edge. 1-5C: 1 or 5 above and CENT below hole. 1P: Elaborate design around center area, 1 PIASTRE in two lines at top and 1931 at bottom of center area. Mint Director's sign left and Engraver's right at bottom edge.

FRENCH INDOCHINA COIN — LEGAL TENDER

SERIES 1923

FI C 8a

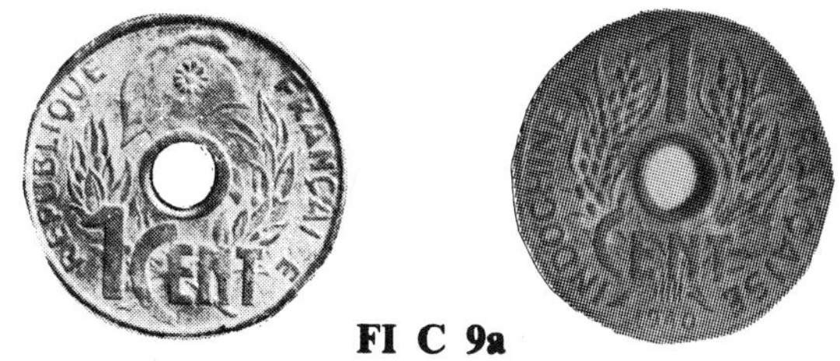

FI C 9a

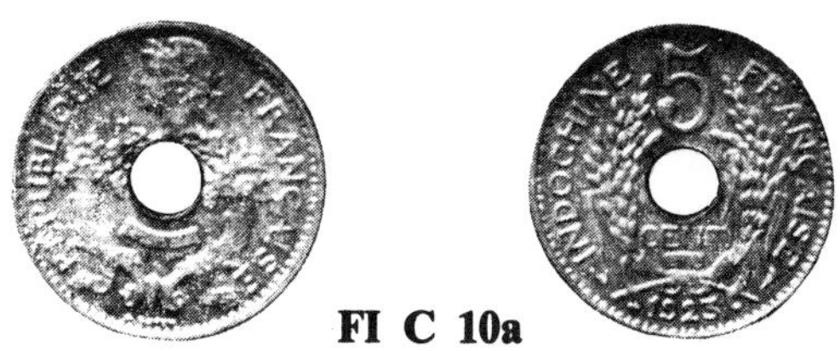

FI C 10a

FI C 11

FRENCH INDOCHINA NOTE — LEGAL TENDER

SERIES 1923

Government: Colony of Cochinchina and Protectorates of Annam, Cambodia, Laos and Tonkin

Governor: Martial-Henri Merlin

Printed at: Bank of France, Paris, France

Designer: Ch. Walhain, Clement Serveau, Georges Duval, Roque and H. Bellery Desfontaines

Engraver: E. Deloche, Rita Dreyfus, Leon Ruffe and E. Gaspe

Dates of Issue: 1923 - 1927

cty, code & number	denomination	width	length	major color	signatures	rarity
FI N 11a	1 Piastre	93mm	148mm	Red	5 and 6	4
FI N 12a	5 Piastres	94	181	Blue	5 and 6	4
FI N 6c	20 Piastres	118	207	Blue	5 and 6	4
FI N 13a	100 Piastres	145	215	Yellow	5 and 6	4
FI N 7e	100 Piastres	145	215	Green	5 and 6	7

Paper: Thin White

Watermark: Head of Vietnamese man

Face: 1-100P: BANQUE DE L'INDOCHINE top center in one line. 1P: Symbolic head of France with helmet left and watermark circle right. CH.WALHAIN FEC. in lower left and E.DELOCHE.SC. in lower right margins. 5P: Symbolic head of France wearing laurel right and watermark area left. CL.SERVEAU FEC in lower left and E.DELOCHE SC in lower right margins. 20P: SAIGON and date printed across center. Symbolic figure of France seated left holding sword and two Orientals right. Watermark area lower left. LEON RUFFE SC. in lower left and GEORGES DUVAL FECIT in lower right margins. 100P:(13a): Three-leg vessel with small lion on cover left, ornate four-post gate across center and watermark circle right. ROQUE FEC. in lower left and RITA SC. in lower right margins. (7e): HAIPHONG and date printed across center. Vietnamese male right with symbolic figure of France behind. H.BELLERY DESFONTAINES DEL. in lower left and L RUFFE SC. in lower right margins.

Back: 1P: BANQUE DE L'INDOCHINE top center in one line and GIAY BAC MOT DONG below. Watermark area lower left and large $1 at lower right. 5P: Peacock standing on stump left, NAM BAC in two lines center and watermark area right. ROQUE FEC. in lower left and RITA SC. in lower right margins. 20P: GEO.DUVAL FEC. in lower left margin. 20 and 100P(7e): Open areas with Vietnamese(Chinese-style) characters describing the notes as issues of the Bank of Indochina, their denomination and that they are payable in silver, and the counterfeiting Article 139 in French. 100P(13a): MOT TRAM BAC in three lines upper left, watermark circle lower left, bust of Dupleix center with name below and head of Ceres lower right.

FRENCH INDOCHINA NOTE — LEGAL TENDER

SERIES 1923

FI N 11a

FI N 12b

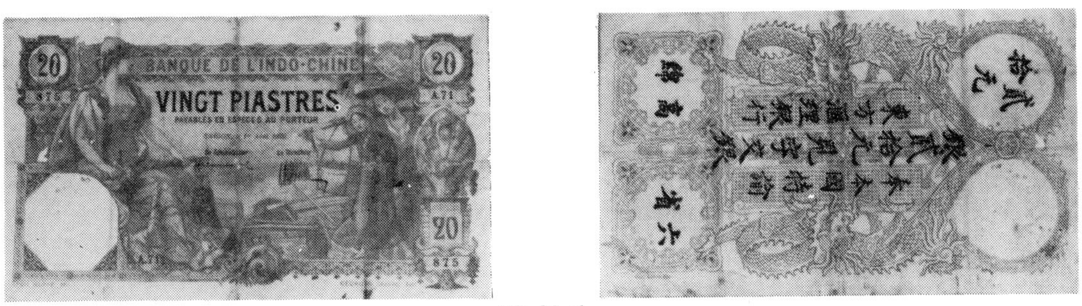

FI N 6c

FI N 13a

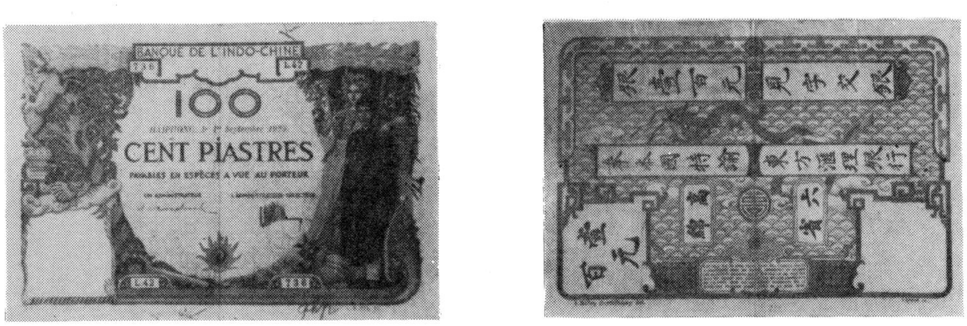

FI N 7e

100 Piastres note(7e) courtesy of Roger Outing.

FRENCH INDOCHINA NOTE — LEGAL TENDER

SERIES 1927

Government: Colony of Cochinchina and Protectorates of Annam, Cambodia, Laos and Tonkin

Governor: Alexandre Varenne

Printed at: Bank of France, Paris, France

Designer: Ch. Walhain, Clement Serveau, Sebastian Laurent and Roque

Engraver: E. Deloche and Rita Dreyfus

Dates of Issue: 1927 - 1936

cty, code & number	denomination	width	length	major color	signatures	rarity
FI N 11b	1 Piastre	93mm	148mm	Red	2 and 6	2
FI N 12b	5 Piastres	94	181	Blue	2 and 6	3
FI N 14	20 Piastres	118	207	Blue	2 and 6	5
FI N 13b	100 Piastres	145	215	Yellow	2 and 6	6

Paper: Thin White

Watermark: Head of Vietnamese man

Face: 1-100P: BANQUE DE L'INDOCHINE top center in one line. 1P: Symbolic head of France with helmet left and watermark circle right. CH. WALHAIN FEC. in lower left and E. DELOCHE.SC. in lower right margins. 5P: Symbolic head of France wearing laurel right and watermark area left. CL.SERVEAU FEC. in lower left and E.DELOCHE SC. in lower right margins. 20P: Symbolic figure of France center with oak trees behind growing up to left and right. Watermark area at lower left. SEB.LAURENT DEL. at lower left and RITA SC at lower right. 100P: Three-leg vessel with small lion on cover left, ornate four-post gate across center and watermark circle right. ROQUE FEC. in lower left and RITA SC. in lower right margins.

Back: 1 and 20P: BANQUE DE L'INDOCHINE top center in one line. 1P: GIAY BAC MOT DONG across top, watermark area lower left and large $1 at lower right. 5P: Peacock standing on stump left, NAM BAC in two lines center and watermark area right. ROQUE FEC. in lower left and RITA SC. in lower right margins. 20P: HAI CHUC BAC in one line at upper left, four-head monument of Buddha center and watermark area at lower right. SEB.LAURENT DEL. at lower left and RITA SC. at lower right edges. 100P: MOT TRAM BAC in three lines upper left, watermark circle lower left, bust of Dupleix center with name below and head of Cere lower right.

FRENCH INDOCHINA NOTE — LEGAL TENDER

SERIES 1927

FI N-11b

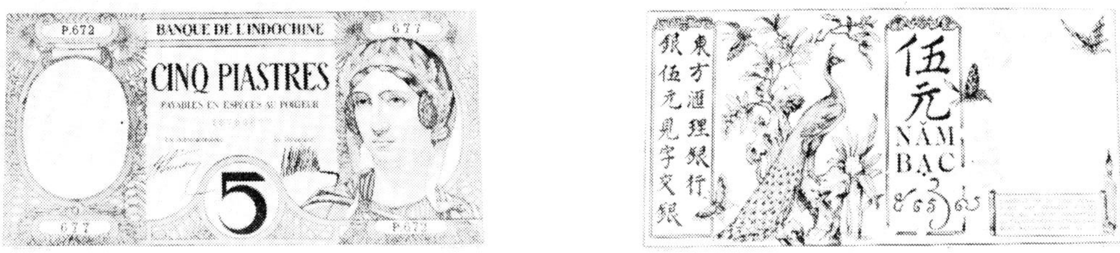

FI N 12b

FI N 14

FI N 13b

FRENCH INDOCHINA NOTE — LEGAL TENDER

SERIES 1933

Government: Colony of Cochinchina and Protectorates of Annam, Cambodia, Laos and Tonkin

Governor: Pierre Pasquier

Printed at: Bank of France, Paris, France

Designer: Sebastian Laurent

Engraver: Hourriez, Rita Dreyfus, and E. Deloche

Dates of Issue: 1933 - 1936

cty, code & number	denomination	width	length	major color	signatures	rarity
FI N 15a	1 Piastre	79mm	127mm	Yellow	6 and 7	6
15b		79	127	Yellow	6 and 7	4
FI N 16a	5 Piastres	91	140	Yellow	6 and 7	4
F16a		91	140	Yellow	6 and 7	—
16b		91	140	Yellow	6 and 7	4
FI N 13c	100 Piastres	145	215	Yellow	6 and 7	6

Paper: Thin White

Watermark: Head of Mercury left(1P) and half-left(5P), and Head of Vietnamese man(100P)

Face: 1-5P: BANQUE DE L'INDOCHINE in one line top center(1P) and bottom center(5P). 1P: Vietnamese woman right, two temples at water's edge center and watermark area left. SEB.LAURENT FEC. in lower left and HOURRIEZ SC. in lower right margins. Blue(a) or red(b) 1 upper right. 5P: Symbolic figure of France left holding a spear and wearing a helmet with watermark area center. SEB.LAURENT FEC. in lower left and E.DELOCHE SC. in lower right margins. Gold wreath inside frame extends into upper right corner(a) or corner is cut(b) with 5 outside frame. Counterfeits(F16a) are known with incorrect serial number for block letter and numbers shown. 100P: Three-leg vessel with small lion on cover left, ornate four-post gate across center and watermark circle right. ROQUE FEC in lower left and RITA SC. in lower right margin.

Back: 1P: GIAY MOT DONG VANG in one line from top center to left. Vietnamese youth left using carrying pole with coconuts in bamboo baskets and another youth on back of water buffalo with three other water buffalo and small monument in background; watermark area right. Chinese characters along left side, Cambodian center(a), and Laotian added(b) below Vietnamese. SEB.LAURENT FEC. in lower left and HOURRIEZ SC. in lower right margins. 5P: Female Cambodian dancer left, watermark area center and four-head monuments of Buddha right. Chinese along right, Cambodian top center(a), and Laotian characters added(b) at upper right. GIAY NAM DONG VANG in one line at bottom center. SEB.LAURENT FEC. in lower left and E.DELOCHE SC. in lower right margins. 100P: MOT TRAM BAC in three lines upper left, watermark circle lower left, bust of Dupleix center with name below and head of Ceres lower right.

FRENCH INDOCHINA NOTE — LEGAL TENDER

SERIES 1933

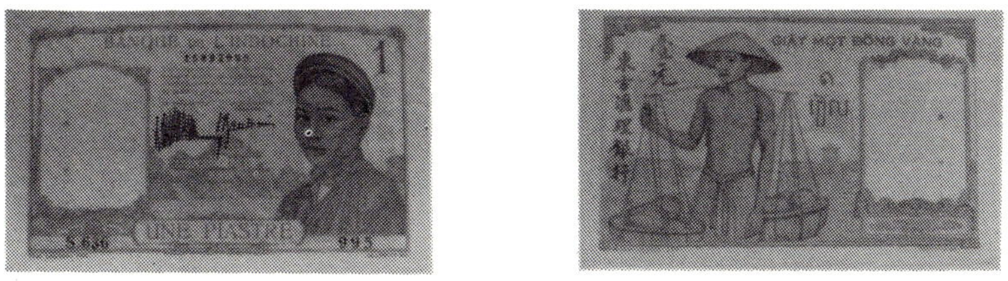

FI N 15a

FI N 16a

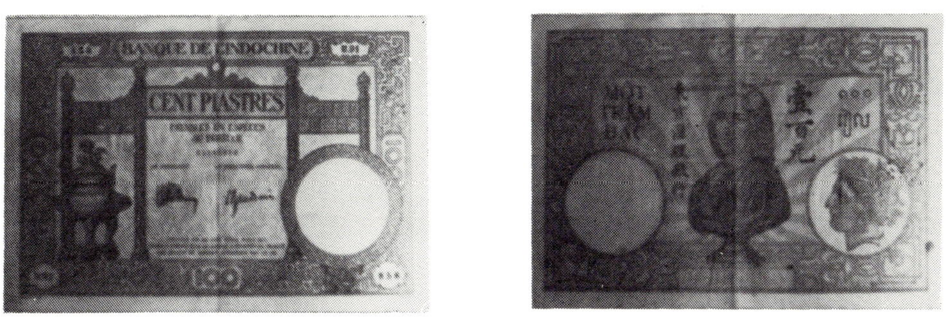

FI N 13c

FRENCH INDOCHINA NOTE — LEGAL TENDER

SERIES 1936

Government: Colony of Cochinchina and Protectorates of Annam, Cambodia, Laos and Tonkin

Governor: Rene Robin

Printed at: Bank of France, Paris, France

Designer: Sebastian Laurent and Roque

Engraver: Hourriez, E. Deloche, J. Piel, and Rita Dreyfus

Dates of Issue: 1936 - 1943

cty, code & number	denomination	width	length	major color	signatures	rarity
FI N 15c	1 Piastre	79mm	127mm	Yellow	8 and 7	2
FI N 16c	5 Piastres	91	140	Yellow	8 and 7	2
FI N 17a	20 Piastres	86	160	Blue	8 and 7	3
FI N 13d	100 Piastres	145	215	Yellow	8 and 7	3
FI N 18a	500 Piastres	103	188	Yellow	8 and 7	4

Paper: Thin White

Watermark: Head of Mercury left(1P), half-left(5P) and full(20 and 500P), and Head of Vietnamese man(100P)

Face: 1-500P: BANQUE DE L'INDOCHINE in one line top or bottom(5P) center and SEB.LAURENT FEC. or ROQUE FEC.(100P) in lower left margin. 1P: Vietnamese woman right, temples center and watermark area left. HOURRIEZ SC. in lower right margin. 5P: Symbolic figure of France left and watermark area center. E.DELOCHE SC. in lower right margin. 20P: Symbolic figure of France center with Athena standing behind and watermark area right. E.DELOCHE-J.PIEL SC. in lower right margin. 100P: Three-leg vessel with small lion on cover left, ornate four-post gate across center and watermark circle right. RITA SC. in lower right margin.

Back: 1-500P: SEB.LAURENT FEC. or blank(100P) in lower left margin. 1 and 500P: HOURRIEZ SC. in lower right margin. 1P: Vietnamese youth with carrying pole left and watermark area right. 5P: Female Cambodian dancer left, watermark area center and stone monuments of Buddha at right. E.DELOCHE SC. in lower right margin. 20P: Symbolic figure of France center with ruins of Angkor Wat right and watermark area left. RITA SC. in lower right margin. 100P: Bust of Dupleix center, head of Ceres right and watermark circle lower left. 500P: Child and figure of France center and watermark area left. HOURRIEZ SC. in lower right margin.

FRENCH INDOCHINA NOTE — LEGAL TENDER

SERIES 1936

FI N 15c

FI N 16c

FI N 17a

FI N 13d

FI N 18a

FRENCH INDOCHINA COIN — LEGAL TENDER

SERIES 1939

Government: Colony of Cochinchina and Protectorates of Annam, Cambodia, Laos and Tonkin **Governor:** Jules Brevie

Minted at: Paris Mint, France and San Francisco Mint, United States

Designer: P. Turin **Engraver:** Lucien Bazor (Wing)

Dates of Issue: 1939 - 1941

cty, code & number	denomination	diameter	thickness	weight	metal	edge	rarity
FI C 12a	10 Cents	18.0mm	1.75mm	3.0grams	Nickel	Reeded	2
12b		18.0	1.75	3.0	Cop-Nic	Reeded	3
12c		18.0	1.75	3.0	Cop-Nic	Reeded	1
FI C 13a	20 Cents	23.0	2.25	7.0	Nickel	Security	2
13b		23.0	2.0	7.0	Cop-Nic	Reeded	1

Metal: Nickel (1.00), and Copper-Nickel (.75 and .25)

Mintmark: None (Paris) or S (San Francisco) **Mint Director's Sign:** Horn or None **Engraver's Sign:** Wing or None

Obverse: REPUBLIQUE FRANCAISE around top edge. Symbolic figure of France facing right wearing Liberty Cap holding branch. P.TURIN at right shoulder and date below at bottom edge. 12b and 13b: Small dots left and right of date.

Reverse: INDOCHINE FRANCAISE around top edge. Sheaf of grain center with 10 or 20 left and CENT right. Mint Director's sign left and Engraver's right of grain at bottom edge, or mintmark right of grain at bottom edge with no signs left or right.

FRENCH INDOCHINA COIN — LEGAL TENDER

SERIES 1939

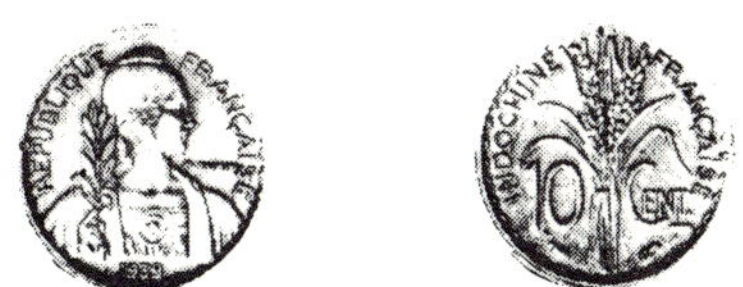

FI C 12c

FI C 13a

FRENCH INDOCHINA NOTE — LEGAL TENDER

SERIES 1939

Government: Colony of Cochinchina and Protectorates of Annam, Cambodia, Laos and Tonkin

Governor: Georges Catroux

Printed at: Imprimerie d'Extreme Orient(IDEO), Hanoi, Tonkin

Designer: G. Barriere

Engraver: Unknown

Dates of Issue: 1939 - 1941

cty, code & number	denomination	width	length	major color	signatures	rarity
FI N 19a	10 Cents	54mm	104mm	Brown	9 and 10	5
19b		54	104	Brown	11 and 10	3
19c		54	104	Brown	11 and 12	1
19d		54	104	Brown	11 and 12	1
FI N 20a	20 Cents	65	104	Green	9 and 10	5
20b		65	104	Green	11 and 10	3
20c		65	104	Green	11 and 12	1
FI N 21a	50 Cents	69	105	Red	9 and 10	6
21b		69	105	Red	11 and 10	3
21c		69	105	Red	11 and 12	2

Paper: Thin White

Watermark: Unidentified or none

Face: 10-50C: GOUVERNEMENT GENERAL DE L'INDOCHINE at top center in two lines. G.BARRIERE lower left and IDEO-HANOI in lower right margins. 10C: Female Cambodian dancer right, ruins of Angkor Wat in background, and stone relief of two female Cambodian dancers left. 19d: Letter(s) preceding serial number. 20D: Bamboo foliage left and right. 50C: Thick leaves left and right.

Back: 10-50C: Counterfeiting Article 139 in French with TRESOR PUBLIC or BANQUE(a). Chinese and Cambodian characters with and without(a) Laotian characters describing denominations. 10C: MUOI XU bottom center in one line. Scene of Cambodian marketplace, several groups of people, and one man riding an elephant. 20C: HAI MUOI XU bottom center in one line. Vietnamese woman wearing conical-shaped hat left, man rowing sampan in standing position with long oar, and jungle scene in background. 50C: NAM MUOI XU bottom lower left in one line. Vietnamese woman with carrying pole right, pond in background, and temple at upper left.

FRENCH INDOCHINA NOTE — LEGAL TENDER

SERIES 1939

FI N 19d

FI N 20a

FI N 21b

FRENCH INDOCHINA NOTE — LEGAL TENDER

SERIES 1941

Government: Colony of Cochinchina and Protectorates of Annam, Cambodia, Laos and Tonkin

Governor: Admiral Jean Decoux

Printed at: Imprimerie d'Extreme Orient(IDEO), Hanoi, Tonkin

Designer: Pham Ngoc Khue

Engraver: Unknown

Dates of Issue: 1941 - 1945

cty, code & number	denomination	width	length	major color	signatures	rarity
FI N 22a	5 Cents	49mm	77mm	Green	11 and 12	2
22b		49	77	Green	11 and 12	1
FI N 23	10 Cents	50	78	Olive	11 and 12	1
FI N 24	20 Cents	55	87	Pink	11 and 12	1
FI N 25	50 Cents	63	96	Green	11 and 12	2

Paper: Thick and thin(22b) white

Watermark: None

Face: 5-50C: GOUVERNEMENT GENERAL DE L'INDOCHINE top center in one line. PHAM NGOC KHUE lower left and IDEO-HANOI lower right margins. 5C: Several vignettes overlapping center. 22a: Letter(s) following serial number and color is lighter. 22b: Letter(s) preceding serial number. 10C: Vignette center with two Phoenix birds above and their tails curling down and around vignette. 20C: Vignette center with two dragons curled around each side. 50C: Vignette center with three bats above and on each side.

Back: 5-50C: Counterfeiting Article 139 in French with TRESOR PUBLIC in center area. Cambodian in upper right, Laotian in lower left, and Chinese characters in lower right corners describing denominations. 5C: NAM XU in upper left corner and vignette center. 10C: MOT HAO in upper left corner and six stalks of grain around center and below. 20C: HAI HAO in upper left corner and stalks of grain around center area. 50C: NAM HAO in upper left corner, ornate frame around center area with grain stalks below.

FRENCH INDOCHINA NOTE — LEGAL TENDER

SERIES 1941

FI N 22a

FI N 23

FI N 24

FI N 25

FRENCH INDOCHINA COIN — LEGAL TENDER

SERIES 1942

Government: Colony of Cochinchina and Protectorates of Annam, Cambodia, Laos and Tonkin **Governor:** Admiral Jean Decoux

Minted at: Osaka Mint (¼C), Japan, and Ecole Pratique d'Hanoi, Tonkin

Designer: Unknown **Engraver:** Unknown

Dates of Issue: 1943 - 1945

cty, code & number	denomination	diameter	thickness	weight	metal	edge	rarity
FI C 14	¼ Cent	20.0mm	1.5mm	2.4grams	Zinc	Smooth	2
U14		20.0	1.5	2.4	Zinc	Smooth	8
F14		20.7	1.5	4.0	Lead	Smooth	—
FI C 15	1 Cent	17.5	1.0	0.5	Aluminum	Smooth	1
FI C 16	5 Cents	21.0	1.5	1.0	Aluminum	Smooth	1

Metal: Zinc (.98 and .02 sulfer), Aluminum (1.00) and Lead (1.00)

Mintmark: None

Obverse: ¼-5C: ETAT FRANCAISE in two lines at top edge, a stalk of grain at each side of 5mm center hole, and date at bottom edge. ¼C: INDOCHINE below hole.

Reverse: ¼C: ¼ at top edge and CENT at bottom edge. Box around center hole with four double lines to single line circle around outer edge. 1C: 1 at top left and CENT at top edge. Two short lines at right of hole. INDOCHINE in straight line at bottom edge. 5C: 5 at top left and CENT at top edge. Two short lines at right of hole. INDOCHINE in curved line at bottom edge.

FRENCH INDOCHINA COIN — LEGAL TENDER

SERIES 1942

FI C 14

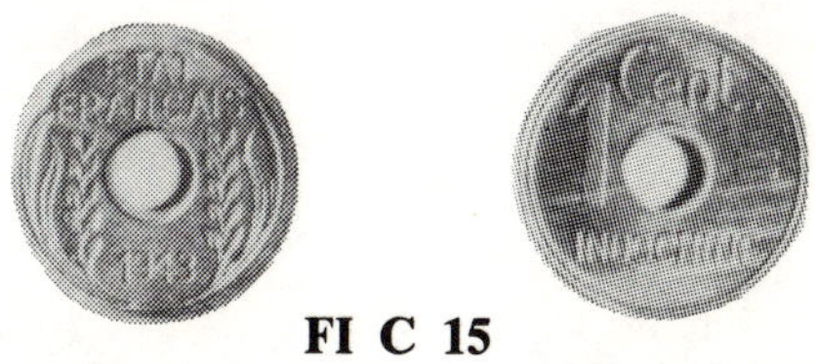

FI C 15

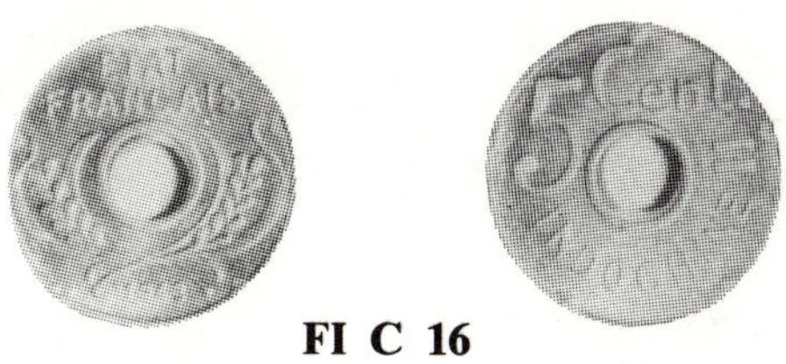

FI C 16

FRENCH INDOCHINA NOTE — LEGAL TENDER

SERIES 1943

Government:	Colony of Cochinchina and Protectorates of Annam, Cambodia, Laos and Tonkin	**Governor:**	Admiral Jean Decoux
Printed at:	Imprimerie d'Extreme Orient(IDEO), Hanoi, Tonkin		
Designer:	Tran Tan Loc, Pham Ngoc Khue and G. Barriere	**Engraver:**	Tran Tan Loc and G. Barriere
Dates of Issue:	1943 - 1945		

cty, code & number	denomination	width	length	major color	signatures	rarity
FI N 26a	1 Piastre	61mm	125mm	Violet	13 and 14	1
26b		61	125	Orange	13 and 14	2
26c		61	125	Green	13 and 14	3
FI N 27a	5 Piastres	73	127	Violet	13 and 14	3
27b		73	127	Green	13 and 14	3
27c		73	127	Dark Green	13 and 14	4
27d		73	127	Dark Green	13 and 14	5
FI N 28a	20 Piastres	75	155	Blue	13 and 14	2
28b		75	155	Brown	13 and 14	3
28c		75	155	Yellow	13 and 14	3
28d		75	155	Pink	13 and 14	7
FI N 29a	100 Piastres	88	174	Lilac	13 and 14	3
29b		88	174	Violet	13 and 14	3
29c		88	174	Green	13 and 14	2
FI N 30a	500 Piastres	76	178	Blue	13 and 14	3
30b		76	178	Green	13 and 14	2

Paper: Thick White

Watermark: Wavy horizontal or vertical lines or none

Face: 1-500P: BANQUE DE L'INDOCHINE in one line across top. 1P: Sampans and junks left and vignette right with $1 inside. TRAN-TANLOC DEL. in lower left margin. 1-100P: IDEO.HANOI in lower right margin. 5P: Wreath of leaves and berries center with 5 inside. 5 and 500P: PHAM-NGOC-KHUE in lower left margin. 20P: Citadel of Hue right and vignette left with 20 inside. TRAN-TANLOC DEL and SC in lower left margin. 100P: Group of Vietnamese, Cambodians and Laotians left and right with woman and child in sampan center. G BARRIERE DEL and SC in lower left margin. 500P: Pavilon, tree, and six Vietnamese irrigating with a three-bucket rope assembly left to right. I.D.E.O.HANOI in lower right margin.

Back: 1P: Cambodian dancer center and TRAN.TANLOC DEL. in lower left margin. 1-100P: IDEO. HANOI in lower right margin. 5P: Pavilon center with trees behind. (27D): Serial number preceded by №. 5,100 and 500 P: PHAN-NGOC-KHUE in lower left margin. 20P: Sitting Buddha center. TRAN-TANLOC DEL and SC. in lower left margin. 100P: Pavilon center inside wreath of leaves and berries and palm fronds across bottom. 500P: Elaborate dragon flying through clouds and I.D.E.O.HANOI in lower right margin.

FRENCH INDOCHINA NOTE — LEGAL TENDER

SERIES 1943

FI N 26a

FI N 27d

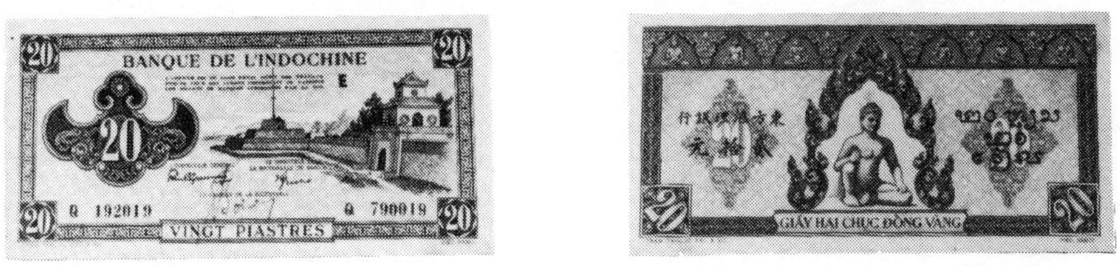

FI N 28a

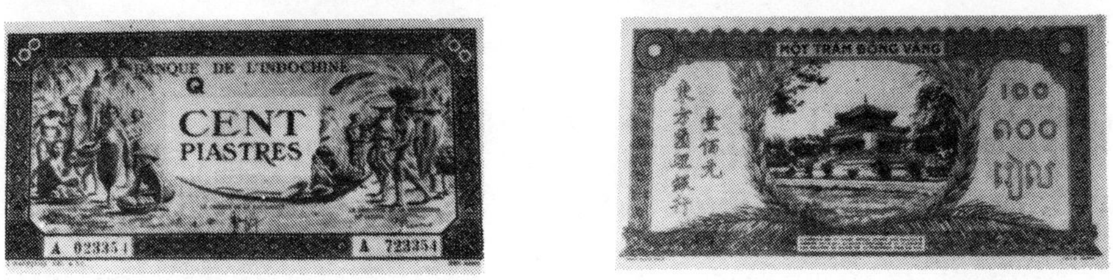

FI N 29c

FI N 30a

FRENCH INDOCHINA COIN — LEGAL TENDER

SERIES 1945

Government: Colony of Cochinchina and Protectorates of Annam, Cambodia, Laos and Tonkin **High Commissioner:** Admiral Georges d'Argenlieu

Minted at: Paris(None), Beaumont le Roger(B) and Castelsarransin(C) Mints, France

Designer: Auguste Barre or P. Turin **Engraver:** Lucien Bazor (Wing)

Dates of Issue: 1945 - 1953

cty, code & number	denomination	diameter	thickness	weight	metal	edge	rarity
FI C 17	5 Cents	18.0mm	1.25mm	0.7grams	Aluminum	Smooth	2
FI C 12d	10 Cents	22.5	1.5	1.3	Aluminum	Smooth	2
FI C 13c	20 Cents	27.0	1.75	2.2	Aluminum	Smooth	2
FI C 5c	50 Cents	29.0	2.5	12.5	Cop-Nic	Reeded	2
FI C 18a	1 Piastre	35.0	2.5	18.0	Cop-Nic	Security	2
18b		35.0	2.5	18.0	Cop-Nic	Reeded	1

Metal: Aluminum (1.00) and Copper-Nickel (.75 and .25)

Mintmark: None, B and C **Mint Director's Sign:** Horn **Engraver's Sign:** Wing

Obverse: 5-50C: REPUBLIQUE FRANCAISE around top edge. 1P: UNION FRANCAISE around top edge. 5-20C and 1P: Symbolic figure of France facing right wearing Liberty cap and holding branch. P. TURIN at right shoulder and date below at bottom edge. 50C: Symbolic figure of France seated holding fasces, anchor behind and grain standing before. Date bottom edge with BARRE left.

Reverse: 5-50C: INDOCHINE FRANCAISE around top edge. 5-20C: Denomination left center of grain and CENT right. 50C: Wreath of leaves and berries around center area tied with a ribbon at the base. 50 CENT in two lines in center area and BRONZE DE NICKEL around bottom edge with Mint Director's and Engraver's signs left and right. 1P: FEDERATION INDOCHINOISE along left and right edge. 1 at top center with PIASTRE below. 5-20C and 1P: Sheaf of grain center. Mint Director's and Engraver's signs left and right of grain at bottom edge. Mintmark, when used, left of Mint Director's sign.

FRENCH INDOCHINA COIN — LEGAL TENDER

SERIES 1945

FI C 17

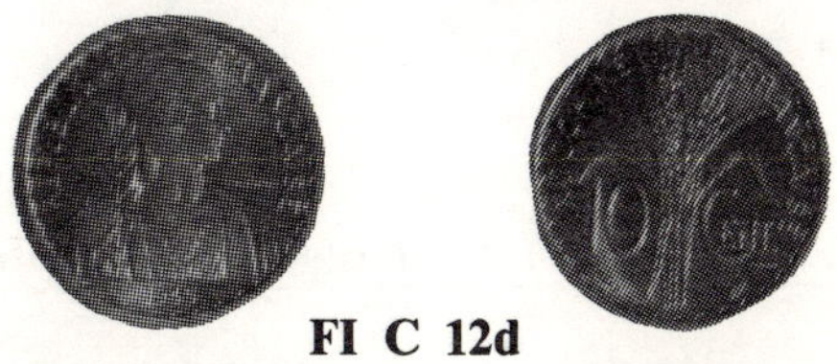

FI C 12d

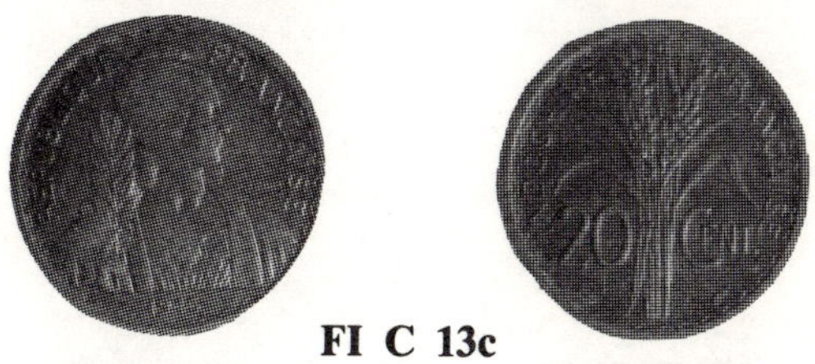

FI C 13c

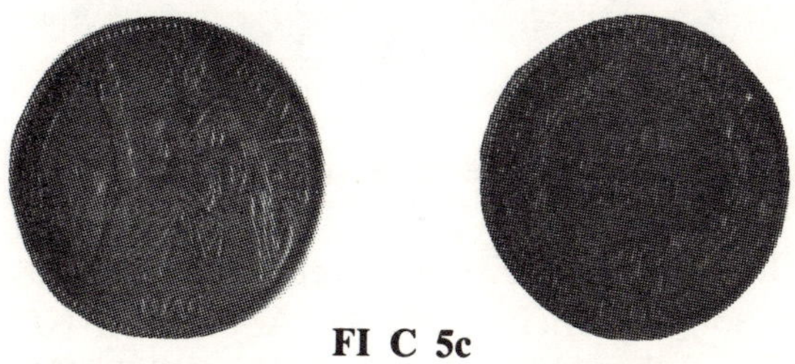

FI C 5c

FI C 18b

FRENCH INDOCHINA NOTE — LEGAL TENDER

SERIES 1945 A

Government: Colony of Cochinchina and Protectorates of Annam, Cambodia, Laos and Tonkin

High Commissioner: Admiral Georges d'Argenlieu

Printed at: American Bank Note Company, New York

Designer: Unknown

Engraver: Unknown

Dates of Issue: 1945 - 1951

cty, code & number	denomination	width	length	major color	signatures	rarity
FI N 31	1 Piastre	64mm	127mm	Brown	13 and 14	3
U31		64	127	Brown	13 and 14	1
FI N 32	50 Piastres	64	153	Green	13 and 14	5
FI N 33	100 Piastres	76	178	Blue	13 and 14	4

Paper: Medium White

Watermark: None, but blue and yellow planchettes across note

Face: 1-100P: BANQUE DE L'INDOCHINE top center to right in one line. 1P: Two Vietnamese rowing sampan in standing position with long oars left. AMERICAN BANK NOTE COMPANY bottom center in margin. Large red letter upper left or lower right of sampan. Letter B(U31) is an unissued note. 50P: Vietnamese woman fanning small bowl of hot coals to singe rice paper kept in three bamboo baskets right. 100P: Row of stone figures along causeway entering Angkor Wat at left.

Back: 1P: GIAY MOT DONG VANG top center in one line. Chinese, Cambodian and Laotian characters left and view of Angkor Wat ruins right to center. AMERICAN BANK NOTE COMPANY bottom center in margin. 50P: GIAY NAM CHUC DONG VANG top center to right in one line. Chinese left and Cambodian and Laotian characters lower right of Cambodian-sculptured panel at Angkor Wat depicting a row of gods holding the body of a serpent described as The Churning of the Sea of Milk across center of note. 100P: MOT TRAM DONG VANG top center to right in one line. Five Vietnamese women using carrying poles with bamboo baskets walking right to left along dike. Chinese characters along right edge with Cambodian and Laotian at lower right.

FRENCH INDOCHINA NOTE — LEGAL TENDER

SERIES 1945 A

FI N 31

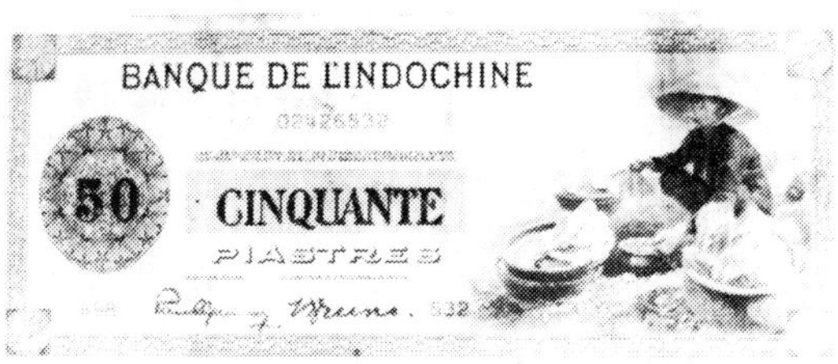

FI N 32

FI N 33

FRENCH INDOCHINA NOTE — LEGAL TENDER

SERIES 1945 B

Government: Colony of Cochinchina and Protectorates of Annam, Cambodia, Laos and Tonkin

High Commissioner: Admiral Georges d'Argenlieu

Printed at: Thomas de la Rue & Company, Ltd., London, England

Designer: Unknown

Engraver: Unknown

Dates of Issue: 1945 - 1946

cty, code & number	denomination	width	length	major color	signatures	rarity
FI N 34	10 Piastres	60mm	141mm	Blue	15 and 16	2
FI N 35	100 Piastres	88	174	Blue	13 and 14	6
F35		88	174	Blue	13 and 14	—

Paper: Medium white and thick(F35) white

Watermark: Head of Laotian woman

Face: 10-100P: BANQUE DE L'INDOCHINE top center in one line and watermark circle lower right. 10P: Ruins of Angkor Wat left to center. 100P: Bank of Indochina building in Saigon center with columns at left and right, and watermark circle lower right. (F35): FAUX overstamped in red across center.

Back: 10-100P: BANQUE DE L'INDOCHINE top center in one line and watermark circle lower left. 10P: GIAY MUOI DONG in one line above Vietnamese using carrying pole with four bunches of rice stalks walking through dried rice paddy center to right. Cambodian characters left and Chinese right of center. 100P: GIAY BAC MOT TRAM DONG in one line above two Vietnamese sampans with double sails in center. Cambodian characters left and Chinese right of center. (F35): FAUX overstamped in red across center.

FRENCH INDOCHINA NOTE — LEGAL TENDER

SERIES 1945 B

FI N 34

FI N 35

FRENCH INDOCHINA NOTE — LEGAL TENDER

SERIES 1946

Government: Colony of Cochinchina and Protectorates of Annam, Cambodia, Laos and Tonkin

High Commissioner: Admiral Georges d'Argenlieu

Printed at: Bank of France, Paris, France

Designer: Sebastian Laurent

Engraver: Hourriez, E Deloche, J. Piel, Rita Dreyfus and E. Gaspe

Dates of Issue: 1946 - 1953

cty, code & number	denomination	width	length	major color	signatures	rarity
FI N 15d	1 Piastre	79mm	127mm	Yellow	15 and 16	2
15e		79	127	Yellow	15 and 16	2
FI N 16d	5 Piastres	91	140	Yellow	15 and 16	2
16e		91	140	Yellow	15 and 16	2
FI N 17b	20 Piastres	86	160	Red	15 and 16	3
FI N 36a	100 Piastres	89	172	Red	15 and 16	2
36b		89	172	Red	15 and 16	2
FI N 18b	500 Piastres	103	188	Red	15 and 16	5

Paper: Thin White

Watermark: Head of Mercury left(1P), half-left(5P) and full(20 and 500P), and Head of Vietnamese man(100P)

Face: 1-500P: BANQUE DE L'INDOCHINE top center(1,20 and 500P), bottom center(5P) in one line and upper right(100P) in two lines. SEB.LAURENT FEC. in lower left margin. 1P: Vietnamese woman right, temples center and watermark area left. HOURRIEZ SC. in lower right margin. 5P: Symbolic figure of France left and watermark area center. E.DELOCHE SC. in lower right margin. 20P: Symbolic figure of France center with Athena standing behind and watermark area right. E.DELOCHE-J.PIEL SC. in lower right margin. 500P: Child and symbolic figure of France center and watermark area right. RITA-J.PIEL SC. in lower right margin.

Back: 1-500P: SEB.LAURENT FEC. in lower left margin. (15e, 16e, 36b and 18b): Laotian characters change shape. 1P: Vietnamese youth with carrying pole left and watermark area right. 1 and 500P: HOURRIEZ SC. in lower right margin. 5P: Female Cambodian dancer left, watermark area center and stone monuments of Buddha at right. E.DELOCHE SC. in lower right margin. 20P: Symbolic figure of France center with ruins of Angkor Wat right and watermark area left. RITA SC. in lower right margin. 100P: Laotian youth with two elephants left, watermark area center and Laotian youth right. E.GASPE SC. in lower right margin. 500P: Child and symbolic figure of France center and watermark area left.

FRENCH INDOCHINA NOTE — LEGAL TENDER

SERIES 1946

FI N 15d

FI N 16d

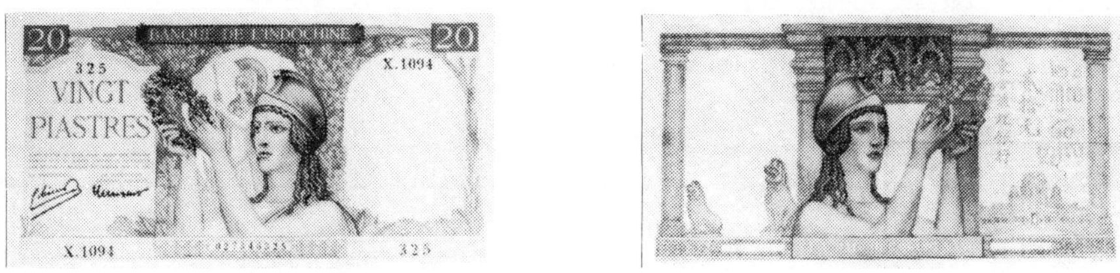

FI N 17b

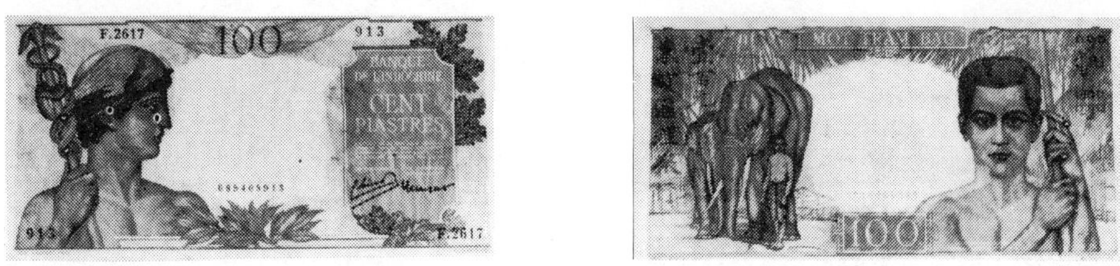

FI N 36b

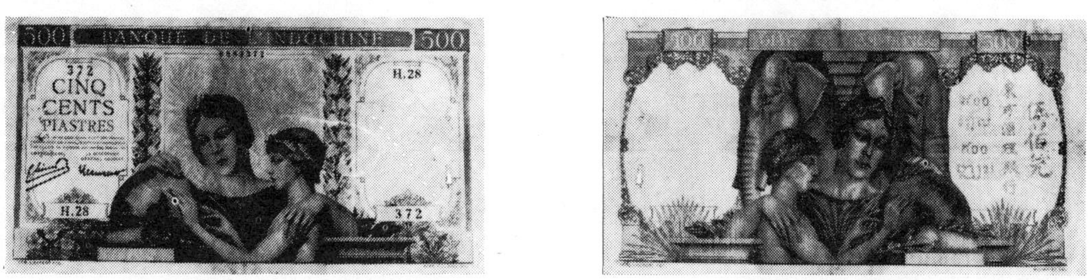

FI N 18b

FRENCH INDOCHINA NOTE — LEGAL TENDER

SERIES 1949

Government: Associated States of Cambodia, Laos and Viet Nam of the French Union

High Commissioner: Leon Pignon

Printed at: Bank of Japan, Tokyo, Japan

Designer: G. Barriere

Engraver: Pham Ngoc Khue

Dates of Issue: 1949

cty, code & number	denomination	width	length	major color	signatures	rarity
FI N 37	1 Piastre	63mm	127mm	Yellow	13 and 14	3
FI N S38	5 Piastres	76	135	Yellow	13 and 14	8
U38	5 Piastres	76	135	Yellow	None	7

Paper: Medium White

Watermark: None

Face: 1-5P: BANQUE DE L'INDOCHINE in one line across top. 1P: Vietnamese woman left with trees behind. Vietnamese farmer plowing with a water buffalo from right to center. G. BARRIERE FEC. in lower left margin. 5P: Four Vietnamese in rice paddy. Boy sitting on grazing water buffalo upper right, farmer plowing with a water buffalo center and house beside trees left. G.BARRIERE DEL. in lower left margin. (S38): SPECIMEN in written style across note from lower left to upper right, a punched hole in center left and right, plate letter W in top left center, zeros for serial number and block number. (U38): No overprinting or punched holes.

Back: 1P: Cambodian girl left and Laotian girl right center. Fruit and vegetables bottom left and right and a tree growing up from center to top left and right. GIAY MOT DONG VANG across top center in one line. G.BARRIERE FEC. in bottom left margin. Chinese characters along right and Cambodian and Laotian characters along left side. 5P: Temple complex from right to center with seven monks from right to left. Many palm trees within and behind complex. GIAY NAM DONG VANG across top center in one line and 5s at each corner. PHAM.NGOC.KHUE in lower right margin. Chinese characters along right and Cambodian and Laotian characters along left side.

FRENCH INDOCHINA NOTE — LEGAL TENDER
SERIES 1949

FI N 37

FI N S38

FI N U38

5 Piastres note(S38) courtesy Clyde M. Reedy.

FRENCH INDOCHINA NOTE — LEGAL TENDER

SERIES 1951

Government: Associated States of Cambodia, Laos and Viet Nam of French Union

Minister: Jean Letourneau

Printed at: Bank of France, Paris, France

Designer: Sebastian Laurent

Engraver: Hourriez

Dates of Issue: 31 December 1951 - 1952

cty, code & number	denomination	width	length	major color	signatures	rarity
FI N 39	1 Piastre	79mm	127mm	Yellow	17 and 18	3

Paper: Thin White

Watermark: Head of Mercury

Face: INSTITUT D'EMISSION DES ETATS DU CAMBODGE, DU LAOS ET DU VIET-NAM top center in two lines and UNE PIASTRE in one line bottom center. Vietnamese woman right, two temples at water's edge center and watermark area left. SEB.LAURENT FEC. in lower left and HOURRIEZ SC. in lower right margins.

Back: Vietnamese youth with carrying pole and coconuts in bamboo baskets left; another youth on back of water buffalo with three other water buffalos and small monument in background. MOT DONG in right center with Laotian and Cambodian characters above and watermark area right. SEB.LAURENT FEC. in lower left and HOURRIEZ SC. in lower right margins.

FRENCH INDOCHINA NOTE — LEGAL TENDER

SERIES 1951

FI N 39

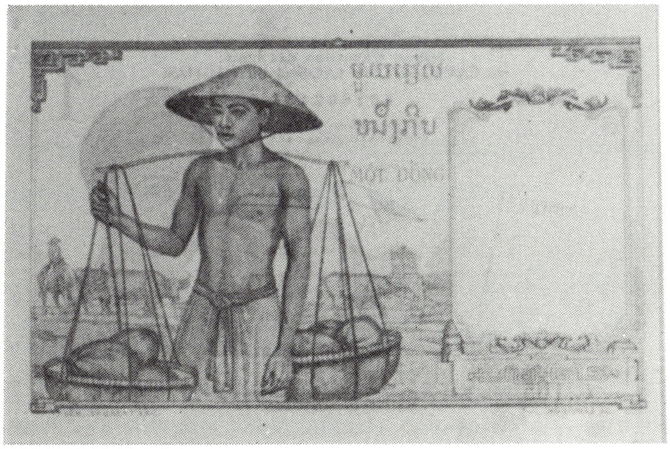

FRENCH CAMBODIA

1863 - 1954

In the early 1860's the Kingdom of Cambodia was being conquered and divided between Siam(Thailand) and Viet Nam. King Norodom I asked for the protection of the French government to save his throne and country. Admiral Lagrandiere, commander of the French naval expeditionary force occupying Saigon and the eastern provinces of what became the Colony of Cochinchina, came to the royal capital of Oudon and signed a Treaty of Protectorate in 1863. A French Resident-Superior, reporting to the French administration in Saigon, was installed in the new capital of Phnom Penh. The country was saved, but several of the northern and western provinces remained under Siam's control.

There were several weights(denominations) of Cambodian copper and silver coins circulating since the 1840's, but barter was the usual form of business transaction in this agricultural economy. The few large transactions and international trade were usually carried out with Mexican 8 Reales or Chinese silver sycee, as was done elsewhere in the many other places of the Far East.

Sometime in the 1870's King Norodom, or his advisors, decided that Cambodia should have a French currency system and commissioned Henri Charles Wurden, an engraver from Belgium, to design the coins. The Cambodian Riel(Tical) was equal to 3 French Francs, which assisted in adoption of the new system. Denominations were struck in bronze 5 and 10 Centimes, silver 25 and 50 Centimes, and silver 1, 2 and 4 Francs coins. They are all dated 1860, for the first year of King Norodom's reign, but probably entered circulation about 1880. The only coins with verified mintages are the 5 and 10 Centimes coins minted at the Heaton Mint, Birmingham, England. The origins of the other coins are still hidden somewhere in France or Cambodia. It is possible that many of the 5 Francs(Ecu) coins that were unsuccessfully circulated in Cochinchina were sent to Cambodia and circulated with these new coins.

On 22 December 1885 Cambodia was made part of the new French Indochina administration formed to govern the new Protectorates of Annam and Tonkin, and the Colony of Cochinchina. In 1890, a branch of the Banque de l'Indochine(Bank of Indochina) was opened in the capital, Phnom Penh. In 1893 Siam renounced all claims to the territory on the left(east) bank of the Mekong River in Cambodia. France put forth claims for the western provinces of Cambodia and after much military and political maneuvering, these provinces were brought under French control in 1907. During this period another branch of the Bank of Indochina was opened in the city of Battambang. During the Siamese control of the Cambodian provinces many copper, billon, and silver coins or tokens were manufactured of Siamese and Cambodian design. These pieces will be fully described in a future volume about the native coins, notes and tokens of Cambodia. The western provinces were reacquired by Thailand in March 1941 with the assistance of the Japanese, but returned to French control after World War II.

Existing 1 Piastre coins of the 1860 design are fantasy type coins and were never meant for circulation in Cambodia. Their design is slightly different than the 1860 coins, their denomination does not fit the Franc currency system, and they first appeared in about 1895. To commemorate the death of the Queen Mother in 1899 more of the 1860-dated were struck with the original dies on minting machines shipped from Europe to establish the Royal Mint in Phnom Penh. The dies were dirty and rusty from long storage in the tropical climate and some were broken striking these new coins. The coins have a grainy appearance, die cracks, and many variations in planchet size and weight. At various times between the original minting and the death of the Queen Mother, sets were also struck in silver or gold as presentation pieces.

With Japanese support, Cambodia declared its independence in March 1945. When the French returned after World War II, the Cambodians negotiated an agreement recognizing limited independence but the French maintained overall control. By 1949 Cambodia was given further independence as a state within the Indochina Federation and the French Union. In 1951, Cambodia and the other states of Indochina were allowed to form their own national banks. Cambodia was allowed to issue coins and bank notes through the Institut d'Emission des Etats du Cambodge, du Laos et du Viet Nam (Issuing Office of the States of Cambodia, Laos and Viet Nam). The Bank of Indochina's privilege of issuing notes was transferred to the Issuing Office in 1951, but it continued to issue its notes until the Issuing Office had sufficient number of notes available for issue.

In 1952 the first bank note for Cambodia was issued in a 1 Piastre(Riel) denomination with King Sihanouk's picture on the face side. Three coins in 10, 20 and 50 Cents(Sen) denominations were issued in 1953 with traditional Cambodian designs. They were followed with a series of bank notes in 1, 5, 10, 100 and 200 Piastres(Riel) denominations. All of the notes had standard face sides for all countries, but the Cambodian back sides had native designs and scenes, as did Laotian and Vietnamese notes. There was a measure of independence and Cambodia issued its own currency through its national bank, but the French continued to control the budget and economy.

Military defeat of the French military forces by the Vietnamese created a series of events which led to the Geneva Convention of 1954 and total independence for Cambodia. The Issuing Office was abolished on 29 December 1954 and an independent National Bank of Cambodia was created on 31 December 1954. Bank of Indochina and Issuing Office notes were exchanged for new independent Cambodia currency until 1956, but the author does not know the final date they were considered legal tender in Cambodia. The 1953 coins continued as legal tender until replaced by 1959 dated coins in exact design except that the Cent denomination was changed to Sen.

FRENCH CAMBODIA COIN — LEGAL TENDER

SERIES 1860

Government: Protectorate of Cambodia (Kingdom) **Governor:** Rear Admiral Baron Victor Duperre

King: S. M. Norodom I

Minted at: Paris, France; Heaton Mint, Birmingham, England; and Royal Mint, Phnom Penh, Cambodia

Designer: Henri Charles Wurden **Engraver:** Henri Charles Wurden

Dates of Issue: Circa 1880 - circa 1904

cty, code & number	denomination	diameter	thickness	weight	metal	edge	rarity
KF C 1a	5 Centimes	25.0mm	1.5mm	5.0grams	Bronze	Smooth	3
1b		25.0	1.5	5.0	Bronze	Smooth	4
KF C 2a	10 Centimes	30.5	2.0	10.0	Bronze	Smooth	2
2b		30.5	2.0	10.0	Bronze	Smooth	3
KF C 3a	25 Centimes	15.3	1.0	1.25	Silver	Smooth	5
3b		15.3	1.0	1.25	Silver	Smooth	5
KF C 4a	50 Centimes	18.4	1.25	2.5	Silver	Reeded	5
4b		18.4	1.25	2.5	Silver	Reeded	5
KF C 5a	1 Franc	23.3	1.55	5.0	Silver	Reeded	5
5b		23.3	1.55	5.0	Silver	Reeded	6
KF C 6a	2 Francs	27.4	2.5	10.0	Silver	Reeded	6
6b		27.4	2.5	10.0	Silver	Reeded	7
KF C 7a	4 Francs	35.0	2.75	20.0	Silver	Reeded	5
7b		35.0	2.75	20.0	Silver	Reeded	4

Metal: Bronze (.85 copper and .15 tin) and Silver (.90 and .10 copper)

Mintmark: None **Mint Director's Sign:** None **Engraver's Sign:** None

Obverse: NORODOM I ROI DU CAMBODGE around top and the date 1860 at bottom edge. Head of King facing left in center with C.WURDEN or C.W(25C) below. Grainy (b) appearance.

Reverse: KINGDOM OF CAMBODIA and denomination in Cambodian sanskrit around top edge and denomination in French at bottom edge. Royal Coat of Arms center.

FRENCH CAMBODIA COIN — LEGAL TENDER

SERIES 1860

KF C 3b

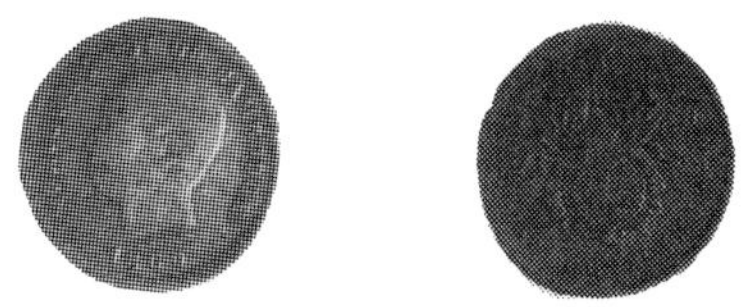

KF C 4b

KF C 5a

KF C 6a

KF C 7b

FRENCH CAMBODIA NOTE — LEGAL TENDER
SERIES 1952

Government: Associated State of French Union **Minister:** Jean Letourneau

Chief of State: King Norodom Sihanouk

Printed at: Chaix, Paris, France

Designer: Unknown **Engraver:** Unknown

Dates of Issue: 1952 - 1953

cty, code & number	denomination	width	length	major color	signatures	rarity
KF N 1	1 Piastre(Riel)	60mm	100mm	Yellow	17 and 19	7

Paper: Medium White

Watermark: None

Face: INSTITUT D'EMISSION DES ETATS DU CAMBODGE DU LAOS ET DU VIET-NAM in two lines across top and serial number at bottom center. Head of King center with elaborate vignette around. UNE PIASTRE at top left and right and 1s at each corner.

Back: Cambodian sanskrit across top center in one line. Elaborate frame and center designs with large circle in center. Cambodian, Laotian and Vietnamese; GIAY MOT DONG, from top, middle to bottom of circle area.

FRENCH CAMBODIA NOTE — LEGAL TENDER

SERIES 1952

KF N 1

FRENCH CAMBODIA COIN — LEGAL TENDER

SERIES 1953

Government: Associated State of French Union **Minister:** Jean Letourneau

Chief of State: King Norodom Sihanouk

Minted at: Paris Mint, France

Designer: Lucien Bazor **Engraver:** Lucien Bazor

Dates of Issue: 1953 - 1959

cty, code & number	denomination	diameter	thickness	weight	metal	edge	rarity
KF C 8	10 Cents (Sen)	23.0mm	1.5mm	1.3grams	Alum-Mag	Smooth	2
KF C 9	20 Cents	27.0	2.0	2.2	Alum-Mag	Smooth	2
KF C 10	50 Cents	31.0	2.25	3.8	Alum-Mag	Smooth	2

Metal: Aluminum-Magnesium (.95 and .05)

Mintmark: None **Mint Director's Sign:** Horn **Engraver's Sign:** Wing

Obverse: Cambodian sanskrit along top and bottom edge. 10C: Ornate Garuda bird at center facing left. 20C: Bound Constitution on urn in center with sun's rays above and water around urn center to bottom. 50C: Royal coat of arms in center.

Reverse: ROYAUME DU CAMBODGE along top edge with date 1953 at bottom edge and Mint Director's sign and Engraver's right of date. Wreath around center area with denomination in one line bottom center and Cambodian sanskrit in two lines at top center within wreath.

FRENCH CAMBODIA COIN — LEGAL TENDER

SERIES 1953

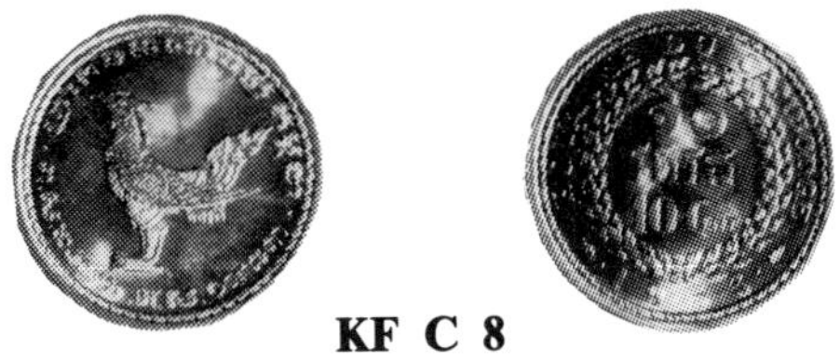

KF C 8

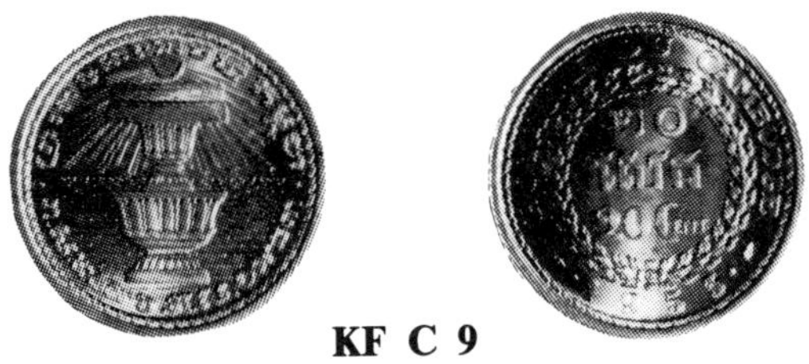

KF C 9

KF C 10

FRENCH CAMBODIA NOTE — LEGAL TENDER
SERIES 1953

Government: Associated State of French Union **Minister:** Jean Letourneau

Chief of State: King Norodom Sihanouk

Printed at: Bank of France, Paris(100 & 200P), France, Thomas de la Rue & Company, Ltd., London(1 & 10P), and Bradbury, Wilkinson & Company, Ltd., New Malden(5P), England

Designer: P. Jouve **Engraver:** J. Piel and G. Beltrand

Dates of Issue: 1953 - 1954

cty, code & number	denomination	width	length	major color	signatures	rarity
KF N 2	1 Piastre(Riel)	80mm	128mm	Blue	17 and 20	5
KF N 3	5 Piastres	84	133	Green	20 and 17	7
KF N 4	10 Piastres	88	139	Yellow	17 and 21	6
KF N 5	100 Piastres	108	172	Green	17 and 20	7
KF N 6	200 Piastres	112	206	Brown	17 and 21	7

Paper: Medium White

Watermark: Head of elephant right and left(100P and 200P)

Face: INSTITUT D'EMISSION DES ETATS DU CAMBODGE DU LAOS ET DU VIETNAM or VIET-NAM(100P and 200P) in three(1P and 10P), one(100P) or two(5P and 200P) lines across top. 1P: Tall trees left, center and right with low green trees behind and watermark area left. 5P: Banana tree left and palm tree right with water toward center from each side and watermark area left. 10P: Elaborate frame with vignette center and watermark area left. 100P: Cambodian, Laotian and Vietnamese girls from left to right on left with trees and flowers in background and watermark area right. 200P: Ornately draped elephant left, two water buffalos right and watermark area center. P.JOUVE FEC left and J.PIEL-G.BELTRAND SC. right bottom margins.

Back: 1P: Floating house left and watermark area right. 5P: Naga(Cobras) halo on pedestal left and watermark area right. 10P: Two Cambodian dancers left and watermark area right. 100P: Scene of Angkor Wat with watermark area in lower left. 200P: Four-head monument of Buddha left and watermark area in center. P.JOUVE FEC left and J.PIEL-G.BELTRAND SC. in right bottom margins.

FRENCH CAMBODIA NOTE — LEGAL TENDER

SERIES 1953

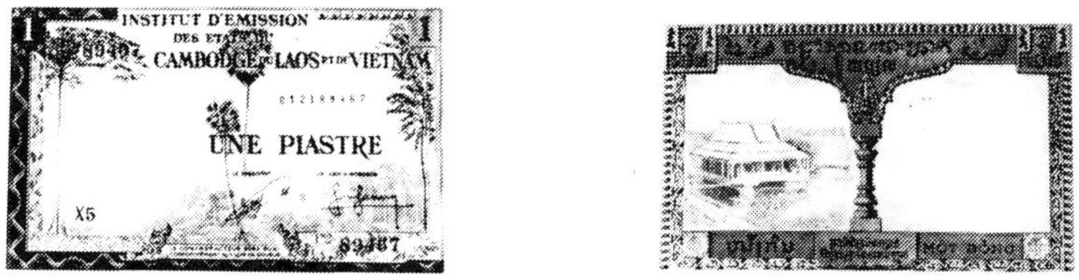

KF N 2

KF N 3

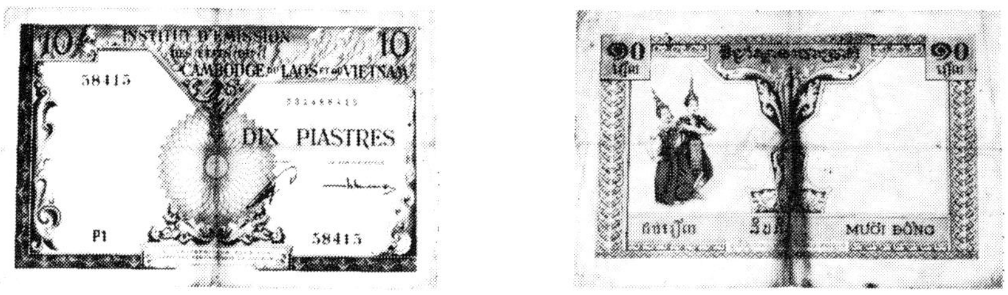

KF N 4

KF N 5

KF N 6

FRENCH LAOS

1893 - 1954

In the late 1880's the French explored the territory west of Viet Nam and north of Cambodia, most of which is now the Kingdom of Laos. At that time it was a loose confederation of principalities and kingdoms with most areas under the control of Siam(Thailand) and few within Viet Nam's influence. In the recent past, Viet Nam and Siam were conquering and dividing Laos much like they did in Cambodia. When the French conquered Viet Nam, Siam took more control of its Laos territory and more over other adjacent areas.

When a Laotian principality northwest of Tonkin was discovered to have been subject to Viet Nam's influence, it was annexed by the French to the Protectorate of Tonkin in 1888. Shortly after, the French visited the King of Luang Prabang, in the royal capital of the same name, to convince him to sign a protectorate in the name of all Laos. In 1893 King Thammathone of Luang Prabang did sign a Treaty of Protectorate, and the French claimed all territory on the left(east) bank of the Mekong River. Siam renounced all claims to Laos, but only after some political and military maneuvering did the Siamese leave in 1902. Some areas were reacquired by Thailand in March 1941 with Japanese support, but they were returned to French control after World War II. The town of Vientiane, south of the royal capital of Luang Prabang, was established as the administrative capital, and a French Resident-Superior was installed there in 1899.

There were several types of Laotian copper and silver bars circulating, but barter was the usual form of business transaction in this agricultural economy. Opium, a widely grown commodity, also served as a form of currency in the remote areas of Laos and is still used today. International trade was with only its close neighbors and was bartered as local transactions, but sometimes Laotian, Siamese, Chinese, and Vietnamese silver bars and coins were exchanged. After 1893, a branch of the Banque de l'Indochine(Bank of Indochina) was opened in Vientiane issuing its notes and the silver French Indochina Piastre and its minor denominations. The silver coins became very popular and were widely used by the people of Laos.

In March 1945 Laos declared its independence with Japanese support. After the Japanese surrender and before the return of the French, a Laotian government issued paper money in several denominations. These notes will be fully described in a future volume about the native coins, notes and tokens of Laos. When the French returned after World War II, the Laotians negotiated an agreement recognizing limited independence, but the French maintained overall control. By 1949 Laos was given further independence as a state within the Indochina Federation and the French Union. In 1951, Laos and the other states of Indochina were allowed to form their own national banks. Laos was allowed to issue coins and banks notes through the Institut d'Emission des Etats du Cambodge, du Laos et du Viet Nam(Issuing Office of the States of Cambodia, Laos and Viet Nam). The Bank of Indochina's privilege of issuing notes was transferred to the Issuing Office in 1951, but it continued to issue its notes until the Issuing Office had sufficient numbers of notes available for issue.

The first three coins of Laos were issued in 1952, all holed and in 10, 20 and 50 Cents(Att) denominations. One bank note was issued in 1952, a 1 Piastre(Kip) denomination, with King Sisavang Vong on the face side. It was followed in 1953 and 1954 with one series of notes in 1, 5, 10, and 100 Piastres(Kip) denominations. All notes had standard face sides for all countries, but the Laotian back sides had native designs and scenes, as did Cambodian and Vietnamese notes. The 200 Piastres(Kip) note was not issued for Laos. In the early 1950's, people living outside the major cities still did not accept paper money, but wanted payment in French Indochina and other silver coins. The small agricultural economy and lack of trust in paper money eliminated the requirement for a 200 Piastres note. Laos had a measure of independence and issued its own currency through its national bank, but the French continued to control the budget and economy.

Military defeat of the French military forces by the Vietnamese created a series of events which led to the Geneva Convention of 1954 and total independence for Laos. The Issuing Office was abolished on 29 December 1954 and an independent National Bank of Laos was created on 31 December 1954. Bank of Indochina and Issuing Office notes were exchanged for new independent Laos currency until 1956, but the author does not know the final date they were considered legal tender in Laos. The 1952 coins continued in circulation to an unknown date as legal tender until inflation eliminated their usefulness.

FRENCH LAOS COIN — LEGAL TENDER

SERIES 1952

Government: Associated State of French Union **Minister:** Jean Letourneau

Chief of State: King Sisavang Vong

Minted at: Paris Mint, France

Designer: Lucien Bazor **Engraver:** Lucien Bazor

Dates of Issue: 1952 - 1959

cty, code & number	denomination	diameter	thickness	weight	metal	edge	rarity
LF C 1	10 Cents (Att)	23.0mm	1.7mm	1.2grams	Alum-Mag	Smooth	1
LF C 2	20 Cents	27.0	2.06	2.1	Alum-Mag	Smooth	1
LF C 3	50 Cents	31.0	2.5	3.7	Alum-Mag	Smooth	1

Metal: Aluminum-Magnesium (.95 and .05)

Mintmark: None **Mint Director's Sign:** Horn **Engraver's Sign:** Wing

Obverse: ROYAUME DU LAOS left and same in Laotian sanskrit along right edge. Hole at center 3mm(10C), 4mm(20C) or 4.5mm(50C) with date 1952 at bottom edge. 10C: Laotian woman's head center facing right. 20C: Royal emblem of three joined elephant heads and forelegs standing on base under seven-tiered parasol center. 50C: Bound Constitution on top of urn center below sun's rays.

Reverse: Twelve leaves facing out from center hole. Date 1952 at bottom edge and same in Laotian sanskrit at top edge. Denomination at lower left and CENTS at lower right and same in Laotian at upper left and right. Mint Director's sign left and Engraver's right of date.

FRENCH LAOS COIN — LEGAL TENDER
SERIES 1952

LF C 1

LF C 2

LF C 3

FRENCH LAOS NOTE — LEGAL TENDER

SERIES 1952

Government: Associated State of French Union **Minister:** Jean Letourneau

Chief of State: King Sisavang Vong

Printed at: Chaix, Paris, France

Designer: Unknown **Engraver:** Unknown

Dates of Issue: 1952 - 1953

cty, code & number	denomination	width	length	major color	signatures	rarity
LF N 1	1 Piastre(Kip)	60mm	100mm	Yellow	17 and 19	5

Paper: Medium White

Watermark: None

Face: INSTITUT D'EMISSION DES ETATS DU CAMBODGE DU LAOS ET DU VIET-NAM in two lines across top and serial number at bottom center. Head of King center with elaborate vignette around. UNE PIASTRE at top left and right and 1s at each corner.

Back: Laotian sanskrit across top center in one line. Elaborate frame and center designs with large circle in center. Laotian, Vietnamese; GIAY MOT DONG, and Cambodian from top, middle to bottom of circle area.

FRENCH LAOS NOTE — LEGAL TENDER
SERIES 1952

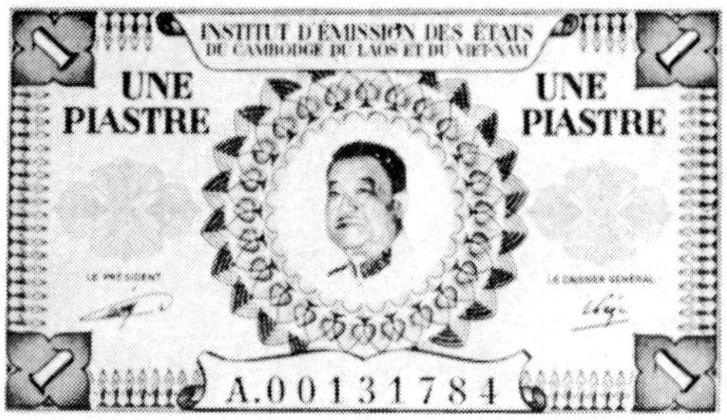

LF N 1

FRENCH LAOS NOTE — LEGAL TENDER

SERIES 1953

Government: Associated State of French Union **Minister:** Jean Letourneau

Chief of State: King Sisavang Vong

Printed at: Bank of France, Paris(100P), France, Thomas de la Rue & Company, Ltd., London(1 & 10P), and Bradbury, Wilkinson & Company, Ltd., New Malden(5P), England

Designer: Unknown **Engraver:** Unknown

Dates of Issue: 1953 - 1954

cty, code & number	denomination	width	length	major color	signatures	rarity
LF N 2	1 Piastre(Kip)	80mm	128mm	Blue	17 and 22	3
LF N 3	5 Piastres	84	133	Green	22 and 17	2
LF N 4	10 Piastres	88	139	Yellow	17 and 22	2
LF N 5	100 Piastres	108	172	Green	17 and 23	4

Paper: Medium White

Watermark: Head of elephant right and left(100P)

Face: INSTITUT D'EMISSION DES ETATS DU CAMBODGE DU LAOS ET DU VIETNAM or VIET-NAM(100P) in three(1P and 10P), one(100P) or two(5P) lines across top. 1P: Tall trees left, center and right with low green trees behind and watermark area left. 5P: Banana tree left and palm tree right with water toward center from each side and watermark area left. 10P: Elaborate frame with vignette center and watermark area left. 100P: Cambodian, Laotian and Vietnamese girls from left to right on left with trees and flowers in background and watermark area right.

Back: 1P: Three-level Wat left and watermark area right. 5P: Buddhist monument left and watermark area right. 10P: Laotian woman facing right at left and watermark area right. 100P: Laotian girl with bowl of flowers right with a Wat center and watermark area left.

FRENCH LAOS NOTE — LEGAL TENDER

SERIES 1953

LF N 2

LF N 3

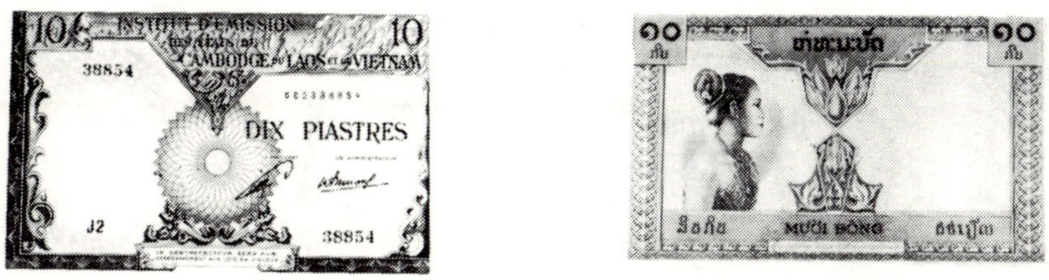

LF N 4

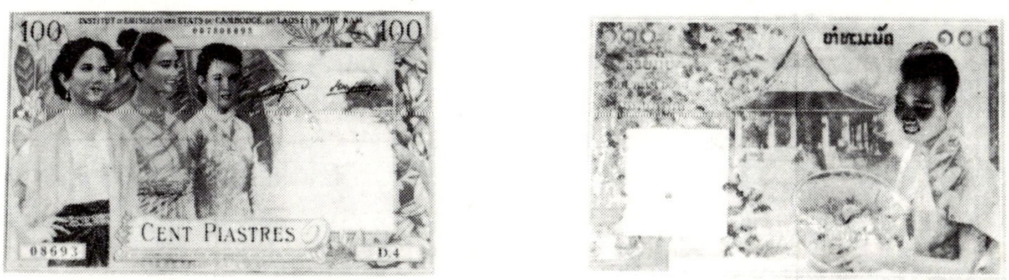

LF N 5

FRENCH VIET NAM

1859 - 1954

Into the late 1850's Viet Nam's treatment of native Catholics and the harassment, imprisonment and killing of European priests created an atmosphere in which some of the Western powers periodically felt obligated to attack Vietnamese positions and rescue the priests. On 18 February 1859, Saigon was captured by a Franco-Spanish squadron, under the command of Admiral Rigault de Genouilly, in a retaliatory attack against Viet Nam, but the French decided to permanently hold Saigon. French military pressure forced the Vietnamese to eventually cede the surrounding provinces and the Colony of Cochinchina was created from the southern delta region of Viet Nam.

From their bases in the Colony of Cochinchina and the Protectorate of Cambodia the French explored the rivers leading north for water routes into China for trading opportunities. Contacts in north Viet Nam caused problems and friction which resulted in an expeditionary force being sent to protect French interests. Military and political events between the Vietnamese and French escalated to such a point that the mandarin(governor) of north Viet Nam was forced to sign a Treaty of Protectorate on 25 August 1883, in the name of the Emperor of Viet Nam. This treaty ended Viet Nam's independence and divided the country into thirds. The north was named Tonkin with a Resident-Superior in Hanoi, the central was named Annam with a Resident-Superior in Hue, and the already established Colony of Cochinchina in the south. Another treaty was signed on 6 June 1884 where Viet Nam officially accepted French control of their internal affairs. During this period of signing treaties, China protested the French takeover of one of its tributary countries. The Chinese and French fought a brief war which resulted in the Chinese withdrawing all claims of Viet Nam's allegiance to China. The last silver seal conferred on the Emperor of Viet Nam was melted in the royal palace at Hue in 1885. The new French Indochina administration was formed to govern the Protectorates of Cambodia, Annam, and Tonkin, and the Colony of Cochinchina.

A branch of the Banque de l'Indochine(Bank of Indochina) was opened in Haiphong issuing its notes and the silver French Cochinchina and new Indochina coins. Branches of the Bank of Indochina were later established throughout Tonkin and Annam. Under the French control, the Vietnamese Emperors were allowed to continue minting their own copper coins, which will be fully described in a future volume about the native coins, notes and tokens of Viet Nam. The French named these coins Sapeques and valued them from 600 to 1200 to the Piastre(Dollar). The French also had a Sapeque coin which was valued at 500 to the Piastre or 1/5th Cent. Vietnamese salaries were based on the French or Vietnamese Sapeque coins depending on their employer. As the exchange value of these currencies rose or fell against each other, many of the Vietnamese suffered from the lower purchasing value of their money. The discontent with these two type coins was a problem which the administration did not need during the building of solid economy in Indochina. Since the French Sapeque was the least acceptable to the people, its issue was discontinued.

The Governor-General of Indochina tasked a study group to create a Sapeque acceptable to the people to replace the Vietnamese coins. A Sapeque coin resulted from this study which closely resembled the Vietnamese coins, but it had a very thin planchet and was made of zinc. The coin was tested in Tonkin and was inscribed with "Protectorat du Tonkin" and "1905" on the obverse and 'One(fraction of 600) Phan General Currency" in Vietnamese(Chinese-Style) characters on the reverse. It was valued at 600 to the Piastre or 1/6th Cent. It was not accepted by the Vietnamese people, and with the previous French Sapeque of 1/5th Cent, both coins were withdrawn from circulation in 1914. Thicker essais and pieforts of the 1905-dated coins were confused, in some references, with the thinner authentic coins considered as counterfeits.

In March 1945, Viet Nam declared its independence with Japanese support and Emperor Bao Dai as its Chief of State. The Japanese retained direct control of Cochinchina, but combined Tonkin and Annam into one Vietnamese state. The Emperor Bao Dai abdicated his throne to a more powerful nationalist movement after they had declared independence on 2 September 1945, naming the country the Democratic Republic of Viet Nam(DRVN), and Ho Chi Minh as president. The DRVN also included Cochinchina, thus completely uniting the country for the first time since the French capture of Saigon in 1859.

When the French returned after World War II, the Vietnamese negotiated an agreement recognizing the independence of the Ho Chi Minh government, but only in the north. The DRVN issued many different coins, notes and tokens throughout Viet Nam. Further negotiation allowed the French to return to the north, but problems and friction resulted in a war between the DRVN and France. During the war the DRVN overprinted Bank of Indochina notes for propaganda purposes as did the French on DRVN notes. Events led to the creation of a French supported State of Viet Nam minus Cochinchina, which was formed into the Republic of Cochinchina, but by 1949 it was merged into the State of Viet Nam. Viet Nam was then given further independence as a state within the Indochina Federation and the French Union, and Bao Dai reclaimed his title as Emperor on 14 June 1949 and returned as its Chief of State. In 1951, Viet Nam and the other states of Indochina were allowed to form their own national banks. Viet Nam was allowed to issue coins and notes through the Institute d'Emission des Etats du Cambodge, du Laos et du Viet Nam(Issuing Office of the States of Cambodia, Laos and Viet Nam). The Bank of Indochina's privilege of issuing notes was transferred to the Issuing Office in 1951, but it continued to issue its notes until the Issuing Office had sufficient numbers of notes available for issue.

In 1952 one bank note was issued in a 1 Piastre(Dong) denomination with Emperor Bao Dai's picture on the face side. Three coins in 10 and 20 Su(Cents), and 50 Xu(Cents) denominations were issued in 1953. Su is the French phonetic spelling of the Vietnamese word Xu. They were followed with a series of notes in 1, 5, 10, 100 and 200 Piastres(Dong) denominations. All of the notes had standard face sides for all countries, but the Vietnamese back sides had native designs and scenes, as did Cambodian and Laotian notes. There was a measure of independence and Viet Nam issued its own currency through its national bank, but the French continued to control the budget and economy.

Military defeat of the French military forces by the Vietnamese created a series of events which led to the Geneva Convention of 1954 and total independence for Viet Nam, but divided at the 17th parallel, with the DRVN in the north and the State of Viet Nam in the south. The Issuing Office was abolished on 29 December 1954 and an independent National Bank of Viet Nam was created in the south on 31 December 1954. The DRVN's national bank had been functioning since 1946. Bank of Indochina and Issuing Office notes were exchanged for Vietnamese currency until 1956, but the author does not know the final date they were considered legal tender in either Viet Nam. The DRVN issued new coins and small denomination notes in 1958, and new coins appeared in the South(now the Republic of Viet Nam) in 1960, to replace the 1953-dated coins.

FRENCH VIET NAM COIN — LEGAL TENDER
SERIES 1905

Government: Protectorate of Tonkin **Governor:** Paul Beau

Emperor: Thanh Thai

Minted at: Paris Mint, France

Designer: Unknown **Engraver:** Henri Patey

Dates of Issue: 1905 - 1914

cty, code & number	denomination	diameter	thickness	weight	metal	edge	rarity
VF C 1	Sapeque(1/6Cent)	25.4mm	0.9mm	2.25grams	Zinc	Smooth	3

Metal: Zinc (1.00)

Mintmark: None **Mint Director's Sign:** Horn **Engraver's Sign:** Torch

Obverse: PROTECTORAT DU TONKIN around top. Date 1905 at bottom edge with Mint Director's sign left and Engraver's right and framed square-like hole (5.8mm) in center.

Reverse: Seven Vietnamese (Chinese-style) characters at bottom, top, right and left meaning One Phan (part of) Six Hundred (of a Piastre) General Currency around square-like hole.

FRENCH VIET NAM COIN — LEGAL TENDER

SERIES 1905

VF C 1

FRENCH VIET NAM NOTE — LEGAL TENDER

SERIES 1952

Government: Associated State of French Union **Minister:** Jean Letourneau

Chief of State: Emperor Bao Dai

Printed at: Chaix, Paris, France

Designer: Unknown **Engraver:** Unknown

Dates of Issue: 1952 - 1953

cty, code & number	denomination	width	length	major color	signatures	rarity
VF N 1	1 Piastre(Dong)	60mm	100mm	Yellow	17 and 19	2

Paper: Medium White

Watermark: None

Face: INSTITUT D'EMISSION DES ETATS DU CAMBODGE DU LAOS ET DU VIET-NAM in two lines across top and serial number at bottom center. Head of ex-Emperor Bao Dai center with elaborate vignette around. UNE PIASTRE at top left and right and 1s at each corner.

Back: Vietnamese; VIEN PHAT HANH across top center in one line. Elaborate frame and center designs with large circle in center. Vietnamese; GIAY MOT DONG, Cambodian and Laotian from top, middle to bottom of circle area.

FRENCH VIET NAM NOTE — LEGAL TENDER

SERIES 1952

VF N 1

FRENCH VIET NAM COIN — LEGAL TENDER

SERIES 1953

Government: Associated State of French Union **Minister:** Jean Letourneau

Chief of State: Emperor Bao Dai

Minted at: Paris Mint, France

Designer: Lucien Bazor **Engraver:** Lucien Bazor

Dates of Issue: 1953 - 1959

cty, code & number	denomination	diameter	thickness	weight	metal	edge	rarity
VF C 2	10 Su(Xu)	23.0mm	1.7mm	1.3grams	Alum-Mag	Smooth	1
VF C 3	20 Su(Xu)	27.0	2.06	2.2	Alum-Mag	Smooth	1
VF C 4	50 Xu	31.0	2.25	3.8	Alum-Mag	Smooth	2

Metal: Aluminum-Magnesium (.95 and .05)

Mintmark: None **Mint Director's Sign:** Horn **Engraver's Sign:** Wing

Obverse: QUOC-GIA VIET-NAM along top edge and date 1953 at bottom with Mint Director's sign left and Engraver's right of date. 10-20S: Three busts of North, Central and South Vietnamese woman from left facing left in center. 50X: Three busts of Vietnamese women facing left (south), center (central) and right (north) in center.

Reverse: 10-20S: VIET-NAM in one line along top edge, sheaf of rice grain center and denomination in lower left and SU in lower right of grain. 50X: VIET NAM in two lines top center, long curling dragons along each side, a large 50 in center with XU below.

FRENCH VIET NAM COIN — LEGAL TENDER
SERIES 1953

VF C 2

VF C 3

VF C 4

FRENCH VIET NAM NOTE — LEGAL TENDER

SERIES 1953

Government: Associated State of French Union **Minister:** Jean Letourneau

Chief of State: Emperor Bao Dai

Printed at: Bank of France, Paris(100 & 200P), France, Thomas de la Rue & Company, Ltd., London(1 & 10P), and Bradbury, Wilkinson & Company, Ltd., New Malden(5P), England

Designer: P. Jouve and W. Fel **Engraver:** J. Piel, A. Marliat and G. Beltrand

Dates of Issue: 1953 - 1954

cty, code & number	denomination	width	length	major color	signatures	rarity
VF N 2	1 Piastre(Dong)	80mm	128mm	Blue	17 and 24	2
VF N 3	5 Piastres	84	133	Green	24 and 17	2
VF N 4	10 Piastres	88	139	Yellow	17 and 24	3
VF N 5	100 Piastres	108	172	Green	17 and 24	2
VF N 6	200 Piastres	112	206	Brown	17 and 24	4

Paper: Medium White

Watermark: Head of Tiger half-right(1 and 5P), right(10P) and full(100 and 200P)

Face: INSTITUT D'EMISSION DES ETATS DU CAMBODGE DU LAOS ET DU VIETNAME or VIET-NAM(100 and 200P) in three(1 and 10P), one(100P) or two(5 and 200P) lines across top. 1P: Tall trees left, center and right with low green trees behind and watermark area left. 5P: Banana tree left and palm tree right with water toward center from each side and watermark area left. 10P: Elaborate frame with vignette center and watermark area left. 100P: Cambodian, Laotian and Vietnamese girls from left to right on left with trees and flowers in background and watermark area right. 200P: Ornately draped elephant left, two water buffalo right and watermark area center. P.JOUVE FEC left and J.PIEL-G.BELTRAND SC. right bottom margins.

Back: 1P: Vietnamese stone lion on pedestal left and watermark area right. 5P: Bust of ex-Emperor Bao Dai left and watermark area right. 10P: The "Candlestick" rock formation north of Haiphong in Ha Long Bay left and watermark area right. 100P: Bao Dai, now Chief of State right, monument center and watermark area left. 200P: Bao Dai left, ornately roofed gate center with watermark area below. W.FEL FEC. left and J.PIEL-A.MARLIAT SC. in right bottom margins.

FRENCH VIET NAM NOTE — LEGAL TENDER

SERIES 1953

VF N 2

VF N 3

VF N 4

VF N 5

VF N 6

FRENCH COCHINCHINA, INDOCHINA, CAMBODIA, VIET NAM, THAILAND AND NETHERLANDS EAST INDIES FRENCH TOKENS

This section includes coin and note tokens from many countries of Southeast Asia. It is really only a trial listing and will likely double and triple in size as research continues by the author and contributors. The only qualifications a token must possess to be described in this section is that some French language or denomination be on it or that it be identified to a French business or French-dominated organization, and that it circulated somewhere in Southeast Asia. The following information will be brief because current research has barely scratched the surface of the books, documents and other records available to the author and contributors.

The tokens are grouped according to a country or area within a country. French Cochinchina tokens are described first with all of them being issued from 1917 to 1922 during the shortage of coins because of World War I. All of the tokens have been listed in one or more references except the Continental Place note tokens which were recently discovered in the American Numismatic Society collection. The French Indochina tokens from the Protectorate of Tonkin were also issued during the shortage of coins from 1920 to 1922. The Maison Vinh Thanh token is assumed to have been issued in Tonkin, but its exact location in one of the Vietnamese areas of Indochina has not been verified.

The French Cambodia tokens of 1875 were probably issued for use within King Norodom's palace in Phnom Penh. The denominations indicate that they were utilized during the same period as the 1860-dated legal tender coins. One set has been reported in silver or silver-plated brass. The 1 Centime token of 1897 is listed in many references. The 1 Centime token with a round center hole is considered by the author to be the token of issue while tokens reported without a hole or a square hole are trails, patterns or unissued specimens. The most commonly given reason for their existence is a shortage of small change in Phnom Penh with several Chinese businessmen sponsoring their manufacture. This token fits into the Centime/Franc currency system and also equals the Sapeque coin of French Cochinchina and Indochina in weight and metal.

The French Viet Nam tokens of 1920 have Sapeque denominations, and because the French Sapeques were withdrawn from circulation in 1914, these tokens must correspond with the Vietnamese copper coins, also called Sapeques by the French. The French coin and note tokens of Thailand are described on page 119. The tokens of the Netherlands East Indies were used by French businesses on the north side of the island of Sumatra during the late 19th century but no firm dates of issue have been established.

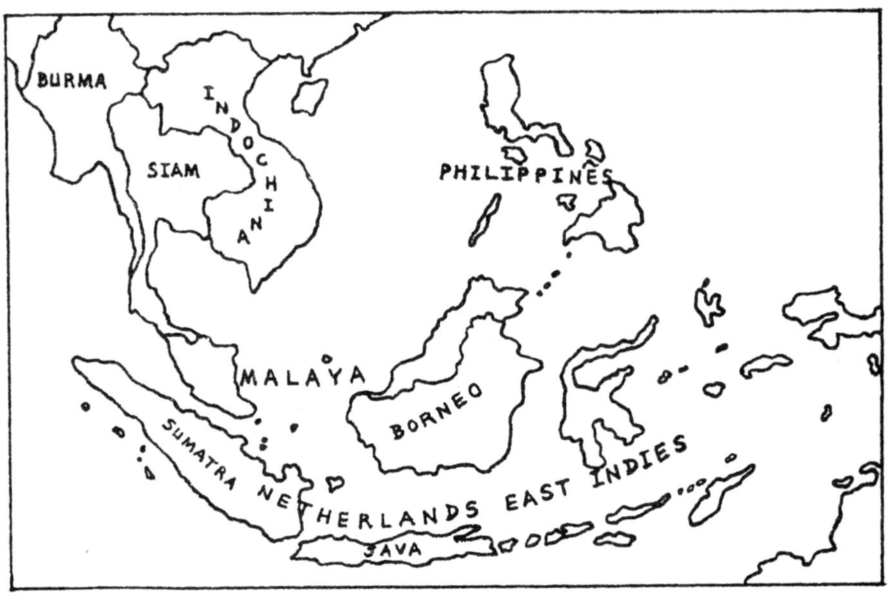

FRENCH COCHINCHINA NOTE — TOKEN

SERIES 1917

Government: Colony of Cochinchina **Governor:** Albert Sarraut

Printed at: Saigon, Cochinchina

Designer: Unknown **Engraver:** Unknown

Dates of Issue: 12 June 1917 - 1922

cty, code & number	denomination	width	length	major color	signatures	rarity
FC NT 1a	6 Cents	Unknown	Unknown	Unknown	Unknown	8
FC NT 1b	12 Cents	Unknown	Unknown	Unknown	Unknown	8
FC NT 1c	17 Cents	Unknown	Unknown	Unknown	Unknown	8
FC NT 1d	30 Cents	Unknown	Unknown	Unknown	Unknown	8

Paper: Unknown

Watermark: Unknown

Face: Boulangerie Bordelaise, Saigon, dated 12 June 1917 is known to be printed on the notes. The design is unknown, but apparently all four denominations are printed on each note. When issued, the denomination is circled, punched out, or otherwise indicated.

Back: Unknown.

Notes are not available for illustration.

FRENCH COCHINCHINA NOTE — TOKEN
SERIES 1919

Government: Colony of Cochinchina **Governor:** Albert Sarraut

Printed at: Imprimerie C. Ardin and Fil, Saigon, Cochinchina

Designer: Unknown **Engraver:** Unknown

Dates of Issue: 30 March 1919 - 1922

cty, code & number	denomination	width	length	major color	signatures	rarity
FC NT 2	5 Cents	60mm	75mm	Yellow	25	8
FC NT 3	10 Cents	51	74	Rose	26	8
FC NT 4	20 Cents	64	91	Green	26	8

Paper: Thin White

Watermark: None

Face: Frame around different background pattern for each denomination. Outside frame is CONTINENTAL vertically at left edge. CONTINENTAL PALACE SAIGON inside frame at top with obverse design of current coin center. B.P. and I.O.Y. with $0.05, $0.10 or $0.20 below, left and right of coin design. Denomination printed over coin design with date at bottom inside frame. CONTINENTAL PALACE top and SAIGON bottom of purple oval-shaped overstamp.

Back: Unframed narrative explaining coin shortage and redemption at hotel cashier top and serial number at bottom left. Signature overstamped in purple ink.

FRENCH COCHINCHINA NOTE — TOKEN

SERIES 1919

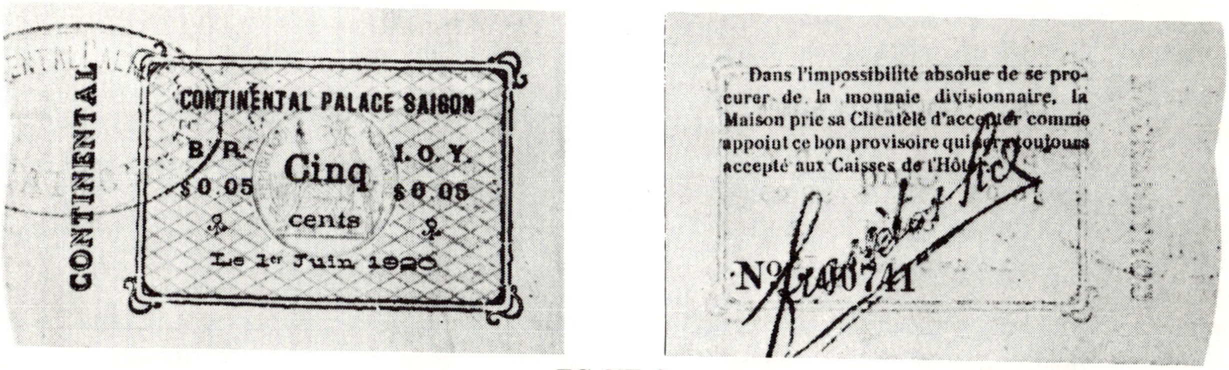

FC NT 2

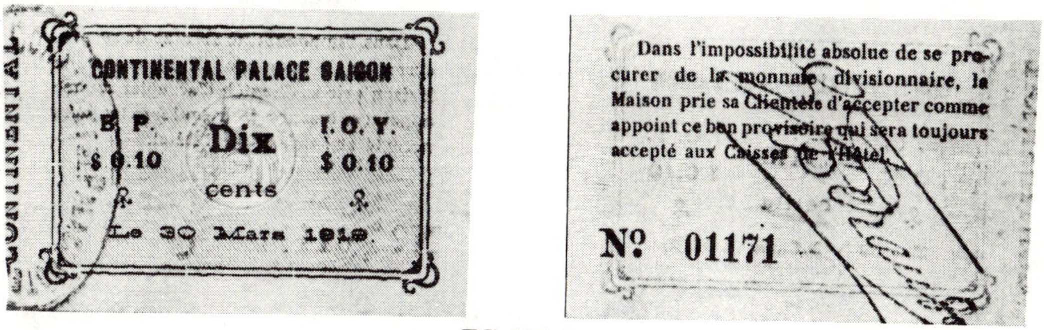

FC NT 3

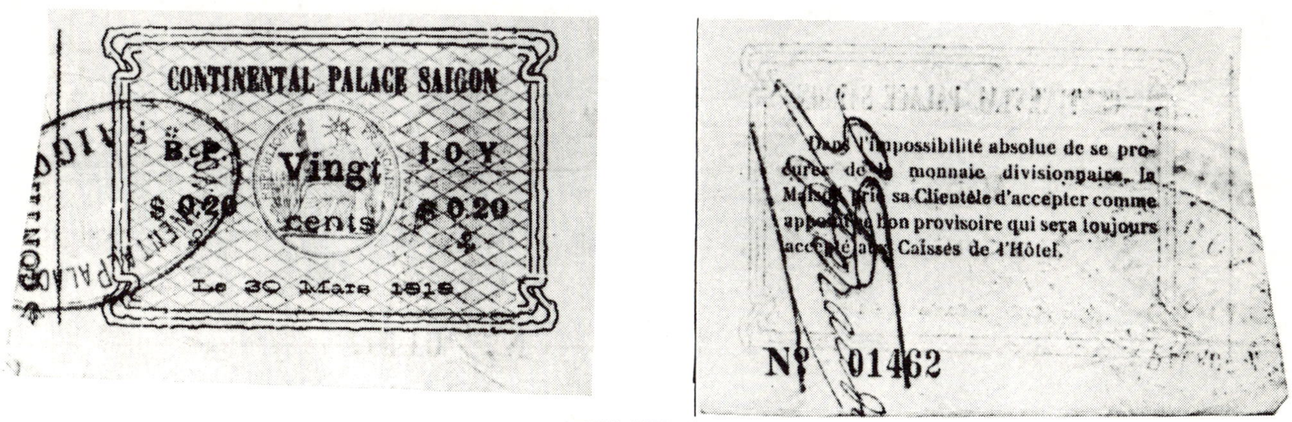

FC NT 4

Notes courtesy of the American Numismatic Society.

FRENCH COCHINCHINA NOTE — TOKEN

SERIES 1920

Government: Colony of Cochinchina **Governor:** Maurice Long

Printed at: Imprimerie C. Ardin and Fil., Saigon, Cochinchina

Designer: Unknown **Engraver:** Unknown

Dates of Issue: 1920 - 1922

cty, code & number	denomination	width	length	major color	signatures	rarity
FC NT 5a	1 Cent	Unknown	Unknown	Unknown	27	8
5b		Unknown	Unknown	Unknown	None	8
FC NT 6a	2 Cents	Unknown	Unknown	Unknown	27	8
6b		Unknown	Unknown	Unknown	None	8
FC NT 7a	3 Cents	52mm	67mm	Black	27	7
7b		52	67	Black	None	8
FC NT 8a	4 Cents	Unknown	Unknown	Unknown	27	8
8b		Unknown	Unknown	Unknown	None	8
FC NT 9a	5 Cents	Unknown	Unknown	Unknown	27	8
9b		Unknown	Unknown	Unknown	None	8
FC NT 10a	10 Cents	Unknown	Unknown	Unknown	27	8
10b		Unknown	Unknown	Unknown	None	8
FC NT 11a	20 Cents	Unknown	Unknown	Unknown	27	8
11b		Unknown	Unknown	Unknown	None	8

Paper: Thick pink(7a)

Watermark: None(7a)

Face: Simple frame with leaf at each corner. STE DES PLANTATIONS DE HONQUAN - COCHINCHINE at top with TICKET POUR UN ACHAT below and DE 0$01, 0$01, 0$03, etc. CENTS below. A L'ECONOMAT DE LA SOCIETE center with UN ADMINISTRATEUR below. Elaborate signature across bottom. SAIGON. IMP. C. ARDIN & FIL. at bottom edge below frame.

Back: Blank.

FRENCH COCHINCHINA NOTE — TOKEN
SERIES 1920

FC NT 7a

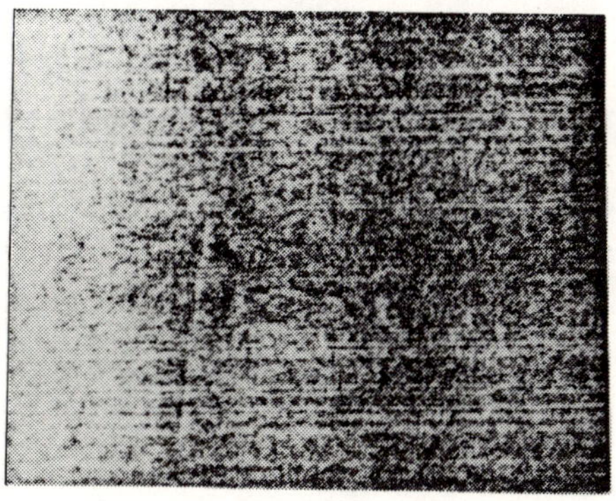

Note courtesy of Pick-Bayerische Hypotheken und Wechsel Bank.

FRENCH INDOCHINA COIN — TOKEN

SERIES 1920

Government: Protectorate of Tonkin **Governor:** Maurice Long

Minted at: Hanoi and/or Haiphong, Tonkin

Designer: Unknown **Engraver:** Unknown

Dates of Issue: 1920 - 1921

cty, code & number	denomination	diameter	thickness	weight	metal	edge	rarity
FI CT 1	20 Cents	Unknown	Unknown	Unknown	Brass	Smooth	8
FI CT 2	5 Cents	Unknown	Unknown	Unknown	Silver	Smooth	8
FI CT 3	10 Cents	Unknown	Unknown	Unknown	Silver	Smooth	8
FI CT 4	25 Cents	Unknown	Unknown	Unknown	Silver	Smooth	8

Metal: Brass and Silver (plated?)

Mintmark: Unknown

Obverse: (1) BRASSERIE DE L'ETOILE(of Hanoi) and (2-4) HOTEL DU COMMERCE(of Haiphong) are parts of unknown designs.

Reverse: Unknown.

Coins are not available for illustration.

FRENCH INDOCHINA NOTE — TOKEN

SERIES 1921

Government: Protectorate of Tonkin **Governor:** Maurice Long

Printed at: Hanoi and/or Haiphong, Tonkin

Designer: Unknown **Engraver:** Unknown

Dates of Issue: 1921 - 18 February 1922

cty, code & number	denomination	width	length	major color	signatures	rarity
FI NT 1	1 Cent	Unknown	Unknown	Unknown	Unknown	8
FI NT 2	2 Cents	Unknown	Unknown	Unknown	Unknown	8
FI NT 3	5 Cents	Unknown	Unknown	Unknown	Unknown	8
FI NT 4	10 Cents	Unknown	Unknown	Unknown	Unknown	8
FI NT 5	20 Cents	Unknown	Unknown	Unknown	Unknown	8
FI NT 6	5 Cents	Unknown	Unknown	Unknown	Unknown	8
FI NT 7	5 Cents	Unknown	Unknown	Unknown	Unknown	8
FI NT 8	20 Cents	Unknown	Unknown	Unknown	Unknown	8
FI NT 9	50 Cents	Unknown	Unknown	Unknown	Unknown	8
FI NT 10	1 Piastre	Unknown	Unknown	Unknown	Unknown	8

Paper: Unknown

Watermark: Unknown

Face: (1-5) SOCIETE FRANCAISE DES CHARBONS DU TONKIN(of Hongay), (6) HOTEL METROPOLE(of Hanoi) dated 18 February 1922, (7) MAISON VINH THANH, KO TCHEOU, and (8-10) KERMESSE CHAVIGON(of Haiphong) dated 1921 are parts of unknown designs.

Back: Unknown.

Notes are not available for illustration.

FRENCH CAMBODIA COIN — TOKEN

SERIES 1875

Government: Protectorate of Cambodia

Governor: Rear Admiral Baron Victor-Auguste Duperre

King: S. M. Norodom I

Minted at: Royal Mint, Phnom Penh, Cambodia

Designer: Unknown

Engraver: Unknown

Dates of Issue: Circa 1875 - 1904

cty, code & number	denomination	diameter	thickness	weight	metal	edge	rarity
KF CT 1	10 Centimes	25.5mm	1.5mm	5.5grams	Brass	Smooth	8
KF CT 2	15 Centimes	25.5	1.5	5.5	Brass	Smooth	8
KF CT 3	20 Centimes	25.5	1.5	5.5	Brass	Smooth	8
KF CT 4	25 Centimes	25.5	1.5	5.5	Brass	Smooth	8

Metal: Brass

Mintmark: None

Obverse: King's initial in one large Cambodian sanskrit character center. CAMPUCHEA around bottom edge and SOMDACH PREA NORODOM PREA CHAU GRUNG around top edge.

Reverse: Denomination center; 25C with eight stars surrounding denomination.

FRENCH CAMBODIA COIN — TOKEN
SERIES 1875

Obverse

KF CT 1

KF CT 2

KF CT 3

KF CT 4

Author's drawings of coins.

FRENCH CAMBODIA COIN — TOKEN
SERIES 1897

Government: Protectorate of Cambodia **Governor:** Paul Doumer

King: S. M. Norodom I

Minted at: Phnom Penh, Cambodia

Designer: Unknown **Engraver:** Unknown

Dates of Issue: 1897 - circa 1914

cty, code & number	denomination	diameter	thickness	weight	metal	edge	rarity
KF CT 5	1 Centime	19.0mm	.75mm	2.0grams	Bronze	Smooth	6

Metal: Bronze (.85 copper and .15 tin)

Mintmark: None

Obverse: ROYAUME DU CAMBODGE around top edge separated with small stars from 1 CENTIME across bottom edge. Framed 3.5mm hole center.

Reverse: Cambodian sanskrit for Kingdom of Cambodia across top edge separated with small diamonds from the denomination in sanskrit at bottom edge.

FRENCH CAMBODIA COIN — TOKEN
SERIES 1897

KF CT 5

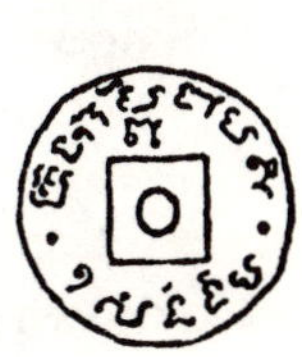

Author's drawing of coin.

FRENCH VIET NAM COIN — TOKEN
SERIES 1920

Government: Protectorate of Tonkin **Governor:** Maurice Long

Emperor: Khai Dinh

Designer: Unknown **Engraver:** Unknown

Dates of Issue: 1920 - 1922

cty, code & number	denomination	diameter	thickness	weight	metal	edge	rarity
VF CT 1	12 Sapeques	Unknown	Unknown	Unknown	Brass	Smooth	8
VF CT 2	15 Sapeques	Unknown	Unknown	Unknown	Brass	Smooth	8
VF CT 3	17 Sapeques	Unknown	Unknown	Unknown	Brass	Smooth	8
VF CT 4	25 Sapeques	Unknown	Unknown	Unknown	Brass	Smooth	8
VF CT 5	30 Sapeques	Unknown	Unknown	Unknown	Brass	Smooth	8
VF CT 6	35 Sapeques	Unknown	Unknown	Unknown	Brass	Smooth	8

Metal: Brass

Mintmark: Unknown

Obverse: SOCIETE MINIERE, TRANG DA is part of an undated and unknown design.

Reverse: Unknown.

Coins are not available for illustration.

THAILAND(FRENCH)

1874 - 1902

The Hong Kong and Shanghai Banking Corporation in 1888, and the Chartered Bank of India, Australia and China in 1893, were allowed to open banks in the royal capital of Bangkok. The Banque de l'Indochine(Bank of Indochina) was allowed to open its bank on 22 February 1897. All three of these banks were privileged to issue bank notes, but they were never considered legal tender. They were acceptable to the businessmen of Bangkok who would trade them for Siamese(Thai) silver bahts at the banks when needed, but outside Bangkok, they were looked on with suspicion and payment had to be in silver bahts. The currency unit of Tical was mistakenly placed on the notes by the European banks as the unit which Siam called a Baht. The original use of Tical is uncertain, but since Baht is correct, it will not be pursued.

The drawings shown in this volume are a combination of sketches drawn by the author while visiting Thailand's National Museum in Bangkok and similar notes issued from other branches of the Bank of Indochina. The small drawings do not allow for the complete details of each note, because many details are unknown to the author. The bank notes on display in the National Museum were unclear photographs. Some additional information about the notes which will be useful to the collector is that the decree line on the 5, 20 and 100 Ticals is DECRET DES 24 JANVIER 1875 ET 20 FEVRIER 1888. The same decrees are printed on the 80 Ticals note in the ribbon-like design at the top center of the note. Bangkok is stamped in the upper left hand corner of the 5 Ticals notes as Saigon and Haiphong were stamped on similar notes for Indochina. Since the notes on display were photographs, the type of paper is assumed to be the same as the Indochina notes of the same period. All of the block letters and numbers, and serial numbers were the letter O or the number zero, and there was no overprinting of the word specimen.

The 5 and 100 Ticals specimens are dated 1898, but the author's research indicates that 1899 was the first year of issue. Thailand withdrew the privilege of issuing bank notes by foreign banks in 1902, and developed bank notes of her own design. The short issuing period of three years and the small area of circulation must have required a very small issue of bank notes, but there was a large Western community in Bangkok, including many French diplomats, military and businessmen. They would have had more contact with these notes than others during 1899 to 1902, and it is assumed that some of them would have been rich enough to save these high denomination bank notes as souvenirs or for their numismatic collections. These collections must have circulation issues of the specimen notes on display in the National Museum? The author estimates that about ten notes of specimens and circulation issues exist for each denomination, but hopes there are more. It is interesting to note that the Bank of Indochina still maintains an office in Bangkok today.

The tokens issued for the Mines de Khaotree are for a French owned mine operating in Siam. King Chulalongkorn reigned from 1868 to 1910, and a similar 2 Att coin of copper or brass was issued during this period, but the token's obverse is an exact copy of the silver 1 Baht coin. The token is assumed to have had been made to fill a shortage of coins in the 2 Att denomination to pay miners. The tokens are well-struck and some appear with proof-like surfaces.

THAILAND(FRENCH) NOTE — TOKEN

SERIES 1898

Dynasty: Chakra

King: Chulalongkorn

Reign Title: Rama V

Printed at: Bank of France, Paris, France

Designer: A. Bramtot, Georges Duval, and Daniel Dupuis

Engraver: J. Robert, A. Leveille and Ch. Wullschleger

Dates of Issue: 1899 - 1902

cty, code & number	denomination	width	length	major color	signatures	rarity
TF NT 1	5 Ticals(Baht)	105mm	140mm	Brown	1 and 2	9
S1		105	140	Brown	1 and 2	8
TF NT 2	20 Ticals	94	181	Green	1 and 2	9
S2		94	181	Green	1 and 2	8
TF NT 3	80 Ticals	118	207	Green	1 and 2	9
S3		118	207	Green	1 and 2	8
TF NT 4	100 Ticals	145	215	Green	1 and 2	9
S4		145	215	Green	1 and 2	8

Paper: Thin White

Watermark: Head of Mercury

Face: 5-100T: BANQUE DE L'INDOCHINE at top in one line. 5T: Symbolic figure of France and Oriental woman seated below and watermark area lower right. DANIEL DUPUIS ET GEORGES DUVAL FEC. in lower left and A.LEVEILLE SC. in lower right margins. 20T: Watermark circle upper left and seated Neptune left. 80T: Elephants standing in front of columns left and right. French woman and cow bottom left and Indian woman and tiger right. Watermark area center. 100T: Vasco de Gama standing in front of column left and Oriental male at right. Ships and boats bottom center.

Back: 5-100T: Various designs with open area with Thai sanskrit characters overprinted describing the notes as issues of the Bank of Indochina, their denomination and that they are payable in Thai silver coins at the bank's building in Bangkok.

THAILAND(FRENCH) NOTE — TOKEN

SERIES 1898

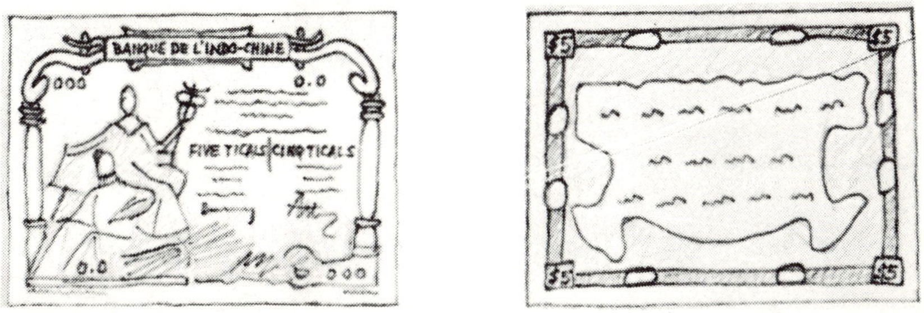

TF NT S1

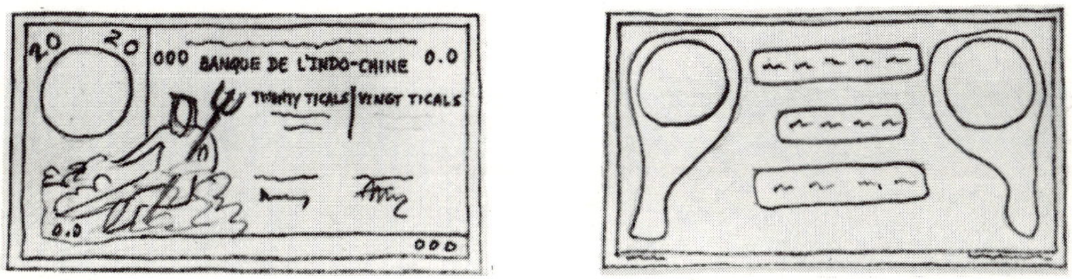

TF NT S2

TF NT S3

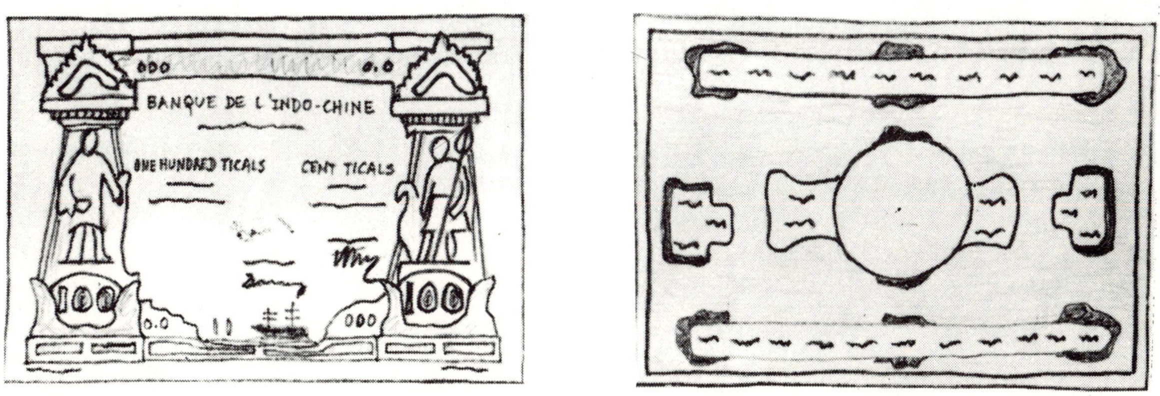

TF NT S4

THAILAND(FRENCH) COIN — TOKEN

Dynasty: Chakra **King:** Chulalongkorn

Reign Title: Rama V

Minted at: Bangkok, Thailand

Designer: Unknown **Engraver:** Unknown

Dates of Issue: Circa 1874 - 1905

cty, code & number	denomination	diameter	thickness	weight	metal	edge	rarity
TF CT 1a	2 Att	31.9mm	2.1mm	10.08grams	Copper	Reeded	6
1b	2 Att	31.9	2.4	10.70	Copper	Reeded	6
1c	2 Att	31.8	2.1	10.50	Brass	Reeded	6

Metal: Copper and Brass

Mintmark: None

Obverse: King Chulalongkorn's head and shoulders in ornate uniform facing left in center. Thai sanskrit completely around outer edge with stylized six-petal flowers separating inscription at lower left and right.

Reverse: MINES DE KHAOTREE around top edge from bottom left to bottom right. GetT with five-pointed stars on left and right at bottom center edge.

THAILAND(FRENCH) COIN — TOKEN

TF CT 1b

NETHERLANDS EAST INDIES(FRENCH) COIN — TOKEN

Government: Colony of East Indies | **Governor:** Unknown

Minted at: Unknown

Designer: Unknown | **Engraver:** Unknown

Dates of Issue: Unknown

cty, code & number	denomination	diameter	thickness	weight	metal	edge	rarity
IF CT 1	20 Cents	25.0mm	Unknown	Unknown	Brass	Smooth	6
IF CT 2	50 Cents	30.0	Unknown	Unknown	Brass	Smooth	6
IF CT 3	1 Dollar	34.0	Unknown	Unknown	Brass	Smooth	6
IF CT 4	20 Cents	Unknown	Unknown	Unknown	Brass	Unknown	6
IF CT 5	1 Dollar	Unknown	Unknown	Unknown	Brass	Unknown	6

Metal: Brass

Mintmark: None

Obverse: (1-3): G. DE MONTBRUN & CO around top edge with stylized five-petal flower at bottom edge. GALLIA SERDANG in two lines center with beaded circle around. (4-5): SOCIETE DES TABACS DE DELI is part of unknown design.

Reverse: (1-3): Denomination in large number(s) center with beaded circle around. BON POUR plus VINGT CENTS, CINQUANTE CENTS or UN DOLLAR around bottom edge separated from three Chinese characters, explaining the denominations by stylized five-petal flowers at left and right. (4-5): Unknown design.

Societe des Tabacs de Deli coins are not available for illustration.

NETHERLANDS EAST INDIES(FRENCH) COIN — TOKEN

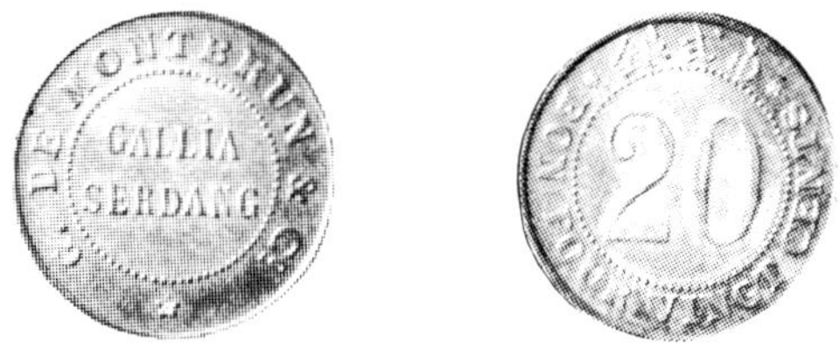

IF CT 1

IF CT 2

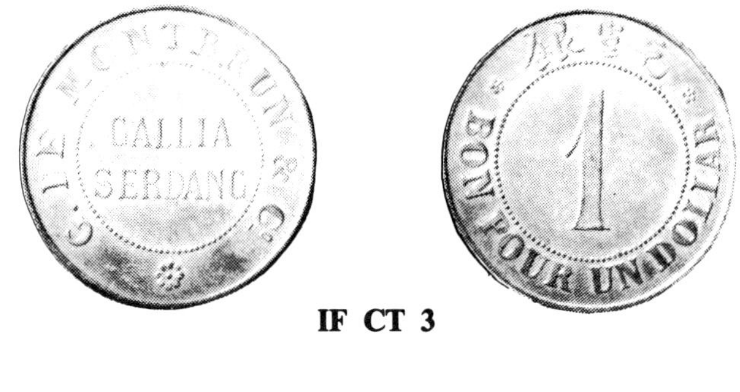

IF CT 3

G. de Montbrun & Co. coins courtesy of Joseph L. Lepczyk.

GUIDEBOOK INTRODUCTION

The Guidebook has three major sections. The first is the signature chart, then a section of dates, values, etc., with a bibliography at the end.

Signature Chart: The signatures shown are only those printed or overstamped on the notes. The handwritten signatures of the cashiers and others are not listed. There are a very large number of these handwritten signatures requiring much more collecting and research before they may be listed. The author's research and information donated by contributors has not revealed the complete or correct name of every signature. Many of the names under the signatures are the interpretation of the author.

The Dates, Values, etc., are grouped by country, colony or protectorate. Within each the legal tender coins, token coins, legal tender notes and token notes are sequentially listed and described as follows:

Cty, Code & Number: The Country, Code and Number are fully explained in the catalog introduction.

Date(*Series*): The date on the coin or note is listed. When there is no date or it is unknown, the Series date is listed. Some notes have only the possible year of the printed date listed. There are many more dates to be discovered and listed, especially for early notes.

Mintmark: A coin mintmark or lack of one is listed for each date. The mintmarks are fully described at the coin descriptions in the catalog. For some French Indochina coins dated 1896 and 1931 the mintmark is followed by a letter in parentheses, the engraver's sign. During these years the engravers changed at the Paris Mint. The author believes that further examination of coins with these dates will reveal that each of them could be listed with two engraver signs.

Issued/Minted or Printed: The number of coins and notes issued will be listed, if known, rather than the total minted or printed. Estimated numbers are italicized..

High Block and High Serial: The highest known block and its serial number, if known, for each date and/or variety of note is listed. Many of the early notes are without block and serial numbers because the available references usually have only basic descriptions of the notes, rarely the date, and almost never the block and serial number. Further collecting and research of all notes will reveal the highest(and lowest) blocks for each date and variety, which will result in more exact numbers issued or printed. The numbering system is described in the French Indochina narrative section of the catalog.

Value: This column will be topped with an abbreviation of the grade; Very Fine(VF), Extremely Fine(EF) or Uncirculated(Unc) for each coin or note valued. Values have generally risen since the first edition, but large numbers of some coin and notes have appeared on the market. The value listings are the most controversial part of any guidebook, but they should be considered only as a guide, and especially where no records exist, the opinion of the author at the exact time he put it on paper. Values are listed in United States dollars. For counterfeit coins or notes the author believes the value should be none. To assign a value to counterfeits only stimulates counterfeiters to create more of them. Only the cost of a dealer's handling plus any possible intrinsic value should be the cost to the collector. After the collector or dealer has studied a counterfeit piece, it should be at least publicized to the numismatic community and/or donated to one of the numismatic organizations that publicizes counterfeits and/or will use them in counterfeit classes to teach others how to detect them.

Bibliography: The publications and periodicals listed are those that have important numismatic and/or historical information, or were the first to publish a significant piece of information, description or illustration of a rare numismatic piece. Further research will reveal additional references with information about the French coins, notes and tokens of Southeast Asia.

SIGNATURE CHART

1. Edouard Delessert
2. Stanislas Simon
3. Denormandrey
4. Baron Hely d'Oissel
5. Albert de Monplanet
6. Robert Thion de la Chaume
7. Paul Baudouin
8. Marcel Bordrige
9. Merry
10. J. Varang
11. L. Fruyua
12. J. Cueur
13. Paul Gannay
14. Edmond Gruno
15. Emile Minost
16. Jean Laurent
17. M. Cusin
18. F. Chuniertuin
19. Uigi
20. Son Sann
21. H. Hiaven
22. K. Junol
23. Ky Huong
24. N. Thien
25. Fraidothel
26. E. Beraud
27. Louis la Courissuray

FRENCH COCHINCHINA

COIN — LEGAL TENDER

cty, code & number	date	mint mark	issued/ mintage	(VF) value
Sapeque(1/10 Cent)				
FC CF H1	1875	K	*1,000,000*	$40.00
Sapeque(1/5 Cent)				
FC C 1	1879	A	20,000,000	9.00
1 Cent				
FC C 2	1879	A	500,000	10.00
	1884	A	444,269	12.50
	1885	A	*255,731*	20.00
10 Cents				
FC C 3	1879	A	400,000	22.50
	1884	A	510,000	20.00
20 Cents				
FC C 4	1879	A	350,000	25.00
	1884	A	320,000	27.50
50 Cents				
FC C 5	1879	A	180,000	35.00
	1884	A	10,000	75.00

NOTE — LEGAL TENDER

cty, code & number	(series) date	issued/ printed	high block	high serial	(VF) value
5 Dollars(Piastres)					
FC N 1a	(1875)	*184,000*	—	—	$1500.00
1b	(1875)	*16,000*	—	—	2500.00
20 Dollars(Piastres)					
FC N 2a	(1875)	*40,000*	—	—	1750.00
	(1875)	*10,000*	—	—	3000.00
100 Dollars(Piastres)					
FC N 3a	(1875)	*8,000*	—	—	3250.00
3b	(1875)	*2,000*	—	—	5000.00

NOTE — TOKEN

cty, code & number	(series) date	issued/ printed	high block	high serial	(VF) value
BOULANGERIE BORDELAISE — SAIGON					
6 Cents					
FC NT 1a	(1917)	*10,000*	—	—	$ 4.50
12 Cents					
FC NT 1b	(1917)	*7,500*	—	—	6.00
17 Cents					
FC NT 1c	(1917)	*6,000*	—	—	7.50
30 Cents					
FC NT 1d	(1917)	*3,500*	—	—	10.00
CONTINENTAL PALACE HOTEL — SAIGON					
5 Cents					
FC NT 2	1 Jun 20	*10,000*	None	00741	4.50
10 Cents					
FC NT 3	30 Mar 19	*7,500*	None	01171	6.00
20 Cents					
FC NT 4	30 Mar 19	*5,000*	None	01462	8.00
SOCIETE DES PLANTATIONS DE HONQUAN					
1 Cent					
FC NT 5a	(1920)	*50,000*	None	None	1.00
5b	(1920)	*40,000*	None	None	1.50
2 Cents					
FC NT 6a	(1920)	*40,000*	None	None	1.50
6b	(1920)	*32,000*	None	None	2.00
3 Cents					
FC NT 7a	(1920)	*32,000*	None	None	2.50
7b	(1920)	*25,000*	None	None	3.00
4 Cents					
FC NT 8a	(1920)	*25,000*	None	None	3.50
8b	(1920)	*17,500*	None	None	3.75
5 Cents					
FC NT 9a	(1920)	*15,000*	None	None	4.00
9b	(1920)	*12,500*	None	None	4.50
10 Cents					
FC NT 10a	(1920)	*7,500*	None	None	6.00
10b	(1920)	*6,000*	None	None	6.75
20 Cents					
FC NT 11a	(1920)	*6,000*	None	None	7.00
11b	(1920)	*5,000*	None	None	8.00

FRENCH INDOCHINA

COIN — LEGAL TENDER

cty, code & number	date	mint mark	issued/ minted	(VF) value
Sapeque				
FI C 1	1887	A	5,000,000	$ 4.00
	1888	A	5,000,000	4.00
	1892	A	1,635,767	5.00
	1893	A	864,233	10.00
	1894	A	2,500,000	3.50
	1897	A	2,828,536	4.00
	1898	A	2,171,464	4.50
	1899	A	5,000,000	4.00
	1900	A	2,656,514	3.50
	1901	A	4,843,486	4.00
	1902	A	2,500,000	3.50
1 Cent				
FI C 2a	1885	A	*3,417,459*	2.50
	1886	A	1,882,541	4.00
	1887	A	2,362,388	3.50
	1888	A	2,564,148	3.50
	1889	A	1,573,364	5.00
	1892	A	2,647,680	3.50
	1893	A	1,852,320	4.00
	1894	A	465,000	10.00
FI C 2b	1895	A	289,747	60.00
10 Cents				
FI C 3a	1885	A	2,040,000	5.00
	1888	A	1,000,000	8.50
	1892	A	200,000	17.50
	1893	A	600,000	9.50
	1894	A	500,000	11.00
	1895	A	600,000	9.50
FI C 3b	1895	A	300,000	15.00
	1896	A(F)	*450,000*	10.00
	1896	A(T)	*200,000*	20.00
	1897	A	900,000	9.00
FI C 3c	1898	A	500,000	10.00
	1899	A	4,100,000	4.50
	1900	A	3,600,000	5.00
	1901	A	2,950,000	6.00
	1902	A	7,050,000	4.00
	1903	A	1,300,000	7.50
	1908	A	1,000,000	8.00
	1909	A	1,000,000	8.00
	1910	A	2,689,161	6.00
	1911	A	2,310,839	6.50
	1912	A	2,500,000	6.50
	1913	A	4,846,605	4.50
	1914	A	2,667,393	6.00
	1916	A	2,000,000	6.50
	1917	A	1,500,000	7.00
	1919	A	1,500,000	7.00
FI C 3d	1920	None	10,000,000	5.00
FI C 3e	1921	A	12,515,504	2.00
	1922	A	22,380,600	1.75
	1923	A	21,755,368	1.75
	1924	A	2,815,659	3.50
	1925	A	4,090,029	3.00
	1927	A	6,470,800	2.50
	1928	A	1,592,863	4.50
	1929	A	5,830,820	2.50
	1930	A	6,607,520	2.50
	1937	None	19,538,220	1.25

cty, code & number	date	mint mark	issued/ minted	(VF) value
20 Cents				
FI C 4a	1885	A	1,280,000	7.50
	1887	A	250,000	27.50
	1892	A	200,000	30.00
	1893	A	200,000	30.00
	1894	A	250,000	27.50
	1895	A	300,000	25.00
FI C 4b	1895	A	250,000	25.00
	1896	A(F)	*200,000*	22.50
	1896	A(T)	*100,000*	30.00
	1897	A	300,000	22.50
FI C 4c	1898	A	250,000	22.50
	1899	A	2,050,000	2.50
	1900	A	1,750,000	3.00
	1901	A	1,375,000	4.50
	1902	A	3,525,000	2.00
	1903	A	675,000	8.00
	1906	A	500,000	11.00
	1909	A	200,000	25.00
(Mule)	1909	A	300,000	20.00
	1911	A	2,339,850	2.00
	1912	A	160,150	30.00
	1913	A	1,251,570	4.00
	1914	A	2,500,000	2.50
	1916	A	1,000,000	5.00
FI C 4d	1920	None	4,000,000	8.00
FI C 4e	1921	A	3,663,041	5.00
	1922	A	5,812,311	4.00
	1923	A	7,109,028	3.00
	1924	A	1,399,682	6.50
	1925	A	2,555,854	6.00
	1927	A	3,244,523	5.50
	1928	A	794,289	7.50
	1929	A	643,750	8.00
	1930	A	5,576,331	4.00
	1937	None	6,116,418	2.00
50 Cents				
FI C 5a	1885	A	40,000	50.00
	1894	A	100,000	35.00
	1895	A	100,000	35.00
FI C 5b	1896	A	110,000	20.00
	1936	None	4,000,000	3.50
FI C 5c	1946	None	32,292,000	3.00
1 Piastre				
FI C 6a	1885	A	799,511	30.00
	1886	A	3,215,771	14.00
	1887	A	3,076,410	14.00
	1888	A	947,615	27.50
	1889	A	1,239,784	22.50
	1890	A	6,108	2750.00
	1893	A	794,723	30.00
	1894	A	1,308,437	22.50
	1895	A	1,782,012	20.00
FI C 6b	1895	A	3,798,452	8.00
	1896	A	11,858,018	7.00
	1897	A	2,511,128	9.00
	1898	A	4,303,953	8.00
	1899	A	4,681,244	7.00
	1900	A	13,318,756	6.00

Fasces(F) and Torch(T) Engraver's Signs.

FRENCH INDOCHINA

COIN — LEGAL TENDER

cty, code & number	(series) date	mint mark	issued/ minted	(VF) value
1 Piastre				
FI C 6b	1901	A	3,150,000	$ 6.50
	1902	A	3,326,554	6.50
	1903	A	10,076,893	6.00
	1904	A	5,750,712	6.25
	1905	A	3,560,882	7.00
	1906	A	10,194,060	6.00
	1907	A	14,061,745	6.00
	1908	A	13,986,340	6.00
	1909	A	9,201,143	6.00
	1910	A	760,718	30.00
	1913	A	3,244,089	7.75
	1921	None	4,850,000	7.75
	1921	H	3,580,000	8.00
	1922	None	1,150,000	20.00
	1922	H	7,420,289	7.00
	1924	A	2,831,349	8.00
	1925	A	2,882,193	7.75
	1926	A	6,382,656	7.25
	1927	A	8,184,076	7.75
	1928	A	5,289,957	15.00
1 Cent				
FI C 7a	1896	A	5,690,262	3.25
	1897	A	11,054,991	1.25
	1898	A	5,000,000	3.50
	1899	A	8,000,000	2.00
	1900	A	3,000,000	4.50
	1901	A	9,750,000	1.50
	1902	A	5,050,000	3.50
	1903	A	8,000,000	2.00
	1906	A	2,000,000	5.00
FI C 7b	1908	A	3,000,000	4.00
	1909	A	5,000,000	3.00
	1910	A	7,703,000	1.75
	1911	A	15,234,000	.50
	1912	A	17,027,300	.50
	1913	A	3,945,392	3.75
	1914	A	11,026,799	.75
	1916	A	1,311,570	5.00
	1917	A	9,761,559	1.00
	1918	A	2,371,528	4.50
	1919	A	9,147,572	1.00
	1920	None	13,290,000	.75
	1920	A	18,305,304	.50
	1921	None	1,610,000	4.25
	1921	A	14,721,854	.75
	1922	Tb	9,475,720	1.00
	1922	A	8,850,117	1.25
	1923	Tb	27,891,109	.50
	1923	A	1,079,468	5.00
	1926	A	11,672,270	.75
	1927	A	3,327,730	4.00
	1930	A	4,682,208	3.25
	1931	A(T)	*3,000,000*	3.00
	1931	A(W)	*2,317,791*	10.00
	1937	A	8,901,992	1.25
1 Cent				
FI C 7b	1938	A	15,499,008	$ .50
	1939	A	15,599,000	.50
½ Cent				
FI C 8a	1935	None	26,365,135	.75
	1936	None	23,634,865	.75
	1937	None	10,243,527	1.25
	1938	None	16,665,473	.75
	1939	None	*16,990,000*	.75
	1940	None	11,218,000	1.25
FI C 8b	1939	None	*315,000*	50.00
	1940	None	185,000	75.00
1 Cent				
FI C 9a	1940	None	1,990,000	4.00
FI C 9b	1940	None	*2,360,000*	2.00
	1941	None	*2,500,000*	2.50
FI C 9c	1940	None	*150,000*	10.00
5 Cents				
FI C 10a	1923	None	1,610,926	2.50
	1924	None	3,389,074	1.50
	1925	None	6,000,000	1.00
	1930	None	4,000,000	1.25
	1937	None	10,000,000	.75
	1938	None	1,480,000	5.00
FI C 10b	1938	None	50,569,000	.50
	1939	None	38,501,000	.50
1 Piastre				
FI C 11	1931	None	13,288,273	8.50
10 Cents				
FI C 12a	1939	None	*16,513,000*	1.00
	1940	None	25,505,000	.75
FI C 12b	1939	None	*328,000*	15.00
FI C 12c	1941	S	30,745,000	.50
FI C 12d	1945	None	40,170,000	.50
	1945	B	9,830,000	1.00
20 Cents				
FI C 13a	1939	None	318,000	10.00
FI C 13b	1939	None	14,676,000	1.50
	1941	S	25,000,000	.75
FI C 13c	1945	None	15,412,000	1.00
	1945	B	6,665,000	1.50
	1945	C	22,423,000	1.00
¼ Cent				
FI C F14	1941	None	—	None
FI C 14	1942	None	*750,000*	7.50
	1943	None	*50,000*	20.00
FI C U14	1944	None	*20*	200.00
1 Cent				
FI C 15	1943	None	*15,000,000*	.50
5 Cents				
FI C 16	1943	None	*10,000,000*	.75
FI C 17	1946	None	28,000,000	.50
	1946	B	22,000,000	.50
1 Piastre				
FI C 18a	1946	None	2,520,000	9.00
	1947	None	*261,250*	25.00
FI C 18b	1947	None	*41,957,500*	2.00

COIN — TOKEN

HANOI — BRASSERIE DE L'ETOILE

cty, code & number	(series) date	mint mark	issued/ minted	(VF) value
20 Cents				
FI CT 1	(1919)	None	*5,000*	3.00

HAIPHONG — HOTEL DU COMMERCE

cty, code & number	(series) date	mint mark	issued/ minted	(VF) value
5 Cents				
FI CT 2	(1919)	None	*25,000*	1.50
10 Cents				
FI CT 3	(1919)	None	*10,000*	2.00
25 Cents				
FI CT 4	(1919)	None	*5,000*	3.00

Torch(T) and Wing(W) Engraver's Signs.

FRENCH INDOCHINA

NOTE — LEGAL TENDER

cty, code & number	(series) date	issued printed	high block	high serial	(VF) value
5 Dollars(Piastres)					
FI N 1a	91	225,000	—	—	$1100.00
FI N 1b	91	25,000	—	—	1350.00
FI N 1c	92	450,000	—	—	1000.00
FI N 1d	92	50,000	—	—	1100.00
FI N 1e	99	675,000	—	—	850.00
FI N 1f	99	75,000	—	—	900.00
FI N 1g	02	900,000	—	—	600.00
FI N 1h	02	100,000	—	—	650.00
FI N 1i	10	1,600,000	—	—	350.00
FI N 1j	10	275,000	—	—	400.00
20 Dollars(Piastres)					
FI N 2a	91	110,000	—	—	1000.00
FI N 2b	91	15,000	—	—	1250.00
FI N 2c	92	225,000	—	—	900.00
FI N 2d	92	25,000	—	—	1000.00
FI N 2e	99	335,000	—	—	750.00
FI N 2f	99	40,000	—	—	800.00
FI N 2g	03	450,000	—	—	500.00
FI N 2h	03	50,000	—	—	550.00
FI N 2i	5 Jun 05	*675,000	F.25	061	250.00
FI N 2j	11 Mar 07	* 75,000	M.33	813	300.00
100 Dollars(Piastres)					
FI N 3a	91	45,000	—	—	1200.00
FI N 3b	91	5,000	—	—	1450.00
FI N 3c	9 May 93	*135,000	Q.6	140	1100.00
FI N 3d	93	15,000	—	—	1200.00
FI N 3e	99	180,000	—	—	950.00
FI N 3f	99	20,000	—	—	1000.00
FI N 3g	9 Mar 03	*225,000	K.10	301	700.00
FI N 3h	03	25,000	—	—	750.00
FI N 3i	15 Mar 07	*450,000	—	—	450.00
	20 Mar 07	25,000	H.19	397	450.00
	29 Mar 07	25,000	—	—	450.00
FI N 3j	6 Jul 03	25,000	W.14	777	675.00
	11 Mar 07	25,000	—	—	500.00
1 Dollar(Piastre)					
FI N 4a	1 Aug 91	925,000	X.23	159	200.00
FI N 4b	1 Aug 91	325,000	—	—	300.00
FI N 4c	1 Aug 91	2,800,000	N.114	581	175.00
FI N 4d	1 Aug 91	950,000	Q.83	712	250.00
FI N 4e	1 Aug 91	16,000,000	E.942	387	50.00
FI N 4f	1 Aug 91	4,000,000	E.738	111	80.00
5 Dollars(Piastres)					
FI N 5a	6 Jun 13	25,000	—	—	70.00
	4 Oct 15	25,000	—	—	60.00
	16 Oct 15	25,000	—	—	60.00
	20 Oct 15	25,000	D.93	070	60.00
	23 Oct 15	25,000	—	—	60.00
	2 Nov 15	25,000	—	—	60.00
	29 Nov 15	20,000	—	—	60.00
	17 Oct 16	25,000	—	—	55.00
	31 Oct 16	25,000	J.160	142	55.00
	8 Nov 16	25,000	C.166	563	55.00
	10 Nov 16	25,000	D.168	315	55.00
FI N 5b	12 Jun 13	25,000	Z.68	668	105.00
	18 Jul 13	25,000	D.72	684	105.00
	27 Nov 15	25,000	C.125	369	95.00
	29 Nov 15	5,000	—	—	95.00

*Total for variety not the date on the line.

FRENCH INDOCHINA

NOTE — LEGAL TENDER

cty, code & number	(series) date	issued/ printed	high block	high serial	(VF) value
5 Dollars(Piastres)					
FI N 5c	12 Jan 20	25,000	M.179	081	$ 50.00
	16 Jan 20	*20,000*	P.183	861	50.00
	6 Feb 20	25,000	B.201	704	45.00
	13 Feb 20	25,000	D.207	412	45.00
	17 Feb 20	25,000	E.210	578	45.00
	23 Feb 20	25,000	—	—	45.00
	8 Mar 20	25,000	—	—	40.00
	9 Mar 20	25,000	P.228	124	40.00
	13 Mar 20	25,000	R.232	508	40.00
FI N 5d	16 Jan 20	*5,000*	—	—	85.00
	27 May 20	*1,300,000*	G.312	952	75.00
20 Piastres					
FI N 6a	19 Apr 17	25,000	N.35	012	85.00
	24 Apr 17	25,000	V.39	764	85.00
	1 May 17	25,000	E.45	576	75.00
	4 May 17	25,000	Z.48	331	75.00
	5 May 17	25,000	R.49	727	75.00
	9 May 17	25,000	J.52	885	75.00
	10 May 17	25,000	N.53	822	75.00
	14 May 17	25,000	T.56	465	75.00
	18 May 17	25,000	R.59	753	75.00
	19 May 17	25,000	M.60	—	75.00
FI N 6b	6 Apr 17	25,000	M.25	670	125.00
FI N 6c	1 Aug 20	1,150,000	W.109	000	50.00
100 Piastres					
FI N 7a	2 Mar 14	25,000	T.5	585	150.00
	4 Mar 14	25,000	H.7	594	150.00
	5 Mar 14	25,000	J.8	360	150.00
	6 Mar 14	25,000	C.9	400	150.00
	3 Apr 19	25,000	V.12	737	100.00
	4 Apr 19	25,000	V.13	939	100.00
	5 Apr 19	25,000	A.14	771	100.00
	7 Apr 19	25,000	Q.15	379	100.00
	8 Apr 19	25,000	J.16	774	100.00
FI N 7b	7 Mar 14	25,000	V.10	512	225.00
	9 Apr 19	25,000	V.17	342	175.00
FI N 7c	5 Jan 20	25,000	T.22	042	85.00
	6 Jan 20	25,000	D.23	522	85.00
	8 Jan 20	25,000	Q.25	058	85.00
	9 Jan 20	25,000	K.26	631	85.00
FI N 7d	10 Jan 20	25,000	—	—	130.00
FI N 7e	1 Sep 25	*50,000*	L.42	736	150.00
10 Cents					
FI N 8a	6 Oct 19	17,000,000	None	8300573	20.00
FI N 8b	6 Oct 19	*25,000,000*	E.96	308	25.00
20 Cents					
FI N 9a	6 Oct 19	6,000,000	None	4640723	45.00
FI N 9b	6 Oct 19	*4,000,000*	—	—	55.00
50 Cents					
FI N 10a	6 Oct 19	3,500,000	None	3346944	70.00
FI N 10b	6 Oct 19	*1,500,000*	—	—	85.00
1 Piastre					
FI N 11a	(1923)	*53,000,000*	T.2860	795	10.00
FI N 11b	(1927)	*45,000,000*	T.4859	695	7.50
5 Piastres					
FI N 12a	(1923)	*11,000,000*	E.425	10604102	15.00
FI N 12b	(1927)	*6,000,000*	P.672	16789677	9.00
100 Piastres					
FI N 13a	(1923)	*575,000*	R.64	01591594	35.00
FI N 13b	(1927)	*500,000*	R.83	02066772	50.00
FI N 13c	(1933)	*300,000*	E.94	02325053	60.00
FI N 13d	(1936)	*4,000,000*	P.255	06364123	25.00

FRENCH INDOCHINA

NOTE — LEGAL TENDER

cty, code & number	(series) date	issued/ printed	high block	high serial	(VF) value
20 Piastres					
FI N 14	(1927)	*2,250,000*	D.189	04703137	$13.00
1 Piastre					
FI N 15a	(1933)	*18,750,000*	Q.666	1664001	15.00
FI N 15b	(1933)	*31,125,000*	D.1163	29053971	7.00
FI N 15c	(1936)	*115,000,000*	D.6408	160178767	3.00
FI N 15d	(1946)	*60,000,000*	W.8931	223274598	2.00
FI N 15e	(1946)	*57,500,000*	A.11279	281950001	1.00
5 Piastres					
FI N 16a	(1933)	*2,250,000*	D.189	04703137	13.00
FI N F16a	(1933)	—	Y.466	22306421	None
FI N 16b	(1933)	*3,750,000*	K.476	11884936	8.00
FI N 16c	(1936)	*20,000,000*	R.1253	31316001	4.00
FI N 16d	(1946)	*92,500,000*	G.4427	110656860	2.00
FI N 16e	(1946)	*12,500,000*	E.5424	135579482	3.00
20 Piastres					
FI N 17a	(1936)	*6,250,000*	M.233	0581132	7.50
FI N 17b	(1946)	*41,250,000*	A.1855	046350001	5.00
500 Piastres					
FI N 18a	(1936)	*575,000*	V.16	0395414	15.00
FI N 18b	(1946)	*1,175,000*	Z.67	1674199	20.00
10 Cents					
FI N 19a	(1939)	*25,000,000*	Y	011307	8.50
FI N 19b	(1939)	*49,000,000*	AQ	977732	1.50
FI N 19c	(1939)	*75,000,000*	EM	926046	1.00
FI N 19d	(1939)	*62,000,000*	BZ425.	540	1.00
20 Cents					
FI N 20a	(1939)	*20,000,000*	I	416037	10.00
FI N 20b	(1939)	*35,000,000*	BB	677553	2.00
FI N 20c	(1939)	*14,000,000*	BZ	882093	1.50
50 Cents					
FI N 21a	(1939)	*10,000,000*	A	572427	15.00
FI N 21b	(1939)	*65,000,000*	BB	008961	2.50
FI N 21c	(1939)	*50,000,000*	DX	385567	2.00
5 Cents					
FI N 22a	(1941)	*17,000,000*	AK	174872	2.50
FI N 22b	(1941)	*120,000,000*	YQ248.	915	1.00
10 Cents					
FI N 23	(1941)	*155,000,000*	HP251.	168	1.00
20 Cents					
FI N 24	(1941)	*107,000,000*	XF248.	560	1.25
50 Cents					
FI N 25	(1941)	*67,000,000*	LH245.	826	1.50
1 Piastre					
FI N 26a	(1943)	*5,000,000*	None	4992991	1.00
FI N 26b	(1943)	*12,000,000*	None	B943002	7.50
FI N 26c	(1943)	*12,000,000*	None	B917109	10.00
5 Piastres					
FI N 27a	(1943)	*2,000,000*	P077	052	7.50
FI N 27a	(1943)	*2,000,000*	V077	453	10.00
FI N 27c	(1943)	*1,650,000*	D066	154	12.50
FI N 27d	(1943)	*1,600,000*	D	1555041	15.00
20 Piastres					
FI N 28a	(1943)	*5,000,000*	V198	945804	10.00
FI N 28b	(1943)	*500,000*	R020	157	7.50
FI N 28c	(1943)	*300,000*	S012	771	7.50
FI N 28d	(1943)	*850,000*	D034	775	50.00
100 Piastres					
FI N 29a	(1943)	*2,050,000*	E082	082	10.00
FI N 29b	(1943)	*250,000*	K010	529	12.50
FI N 29c	(1943)	*575,000*	A023	354	5.00
500 Piastres					
FI N 30a	(1943)	*600,000*	A024	533	15.00
FI N 30b	(1943)	*400,000*	K016	140	10.00
1 Piastre					
FI N 31	(1945)	*21,000,000*	P.1035	25864810	2.50
FI N U31	(1945)	*5,000,000*	M.319	07961581	1.00
50 Piastres					
FI N 32	(1945)	*5,000,000*	A.197	04900821	5.00

FRENCH INDOCHINA

NOTE — LEGAL TENDER

cty, code & number	(series) date	issued/ printed	high block	high serial	(VF) value
100 Piastres					
FI N 33	(1945)	*5,000,000*	P.196	04889301	$ 10.00
10 Piastres					
FI N 34	(1945)	*38,000,000*	AL	074804	1.50
100 Piastres					
FI N 35	(1945)	*5,500,000*	W.218	0858	25.00
FI N F35	(1945)	—	K.563	0987	None
100 Piastres					
FI N 36a	(1946)	*45,000,000*	P.1734	43339408	5.00
FI N 36b	(1946)	*37,500,000*	G.3282	082032935	5.00
1 Piastre					
FI N 37	(1949)	*10,000,000*	354M	8835396	7.50
5 Piastres					
FI N S38	(1949)	*5*	000.W	0000000	175.00
FI N U38	(1949)	*20*	None	None	100.00
1 Piastre					
FI N 39	(1951)	*15,000,000*	E.582	014529553	1.50

NOTE — TOKEN

	HON GAY — SOCIETE FRANCAISE DES CHARBONS DU TONKIN				
1 Cent					
FI NT 1	(1921)	*75,000*	—	—	1.00
2 Cents					
FI NT 2	(1921)	*50,000*	—	—	1.25
5 Cents					
FI NT 3	(1921)	*25,000*	—	—	1.50
10 Cents					
FI NT 4	(1921)	*10,000*	—	—	2.00
20 Cents					
FI NT 5	(1921)	*7,500*	—	—	3.00
	HANOI — HOTEL METROPOLE				
5 Cents					
FI NT 6	18 Feb 22	*25,000*	—	—	1.50
	VINH THANH — MAISON VINH THANH(KO TCHEOU)				
5 Cents					
FI NT 7	(1921)	*25,000*	—	—	1.50
	HAIPHONG — KERMESSE CHAVIGON				
20 Cents					
FI NT 8	21	*7,500*	—	—	3.00
50 Cents					
FI NT 9	21	*5,000*	—	—	5.00
1 Piastre					
FI NT 10	21	*2,500*	—	—	10.00

FRENCH CAMBODIA

COIN — LEGAL TENDER

cty, code & number	(series) date	mint mark	issued/ minted	(VF) value
5 Centimes				
KF C 1a	1860	None	11,465,000	12.50
1b	1860	None	*500,000*	10.00
10 Centimes				
KF C 2a	1860	None	10,265,000	15.00
2b	1860	None	*440,000*	12.50
25 Centimes				
KF C 3a	1860	None	*175,000*	17.50
3b	1860	None	*255,000*	15.00
50 Centimes				
KF C 4a	1860	None	*150,000*	25.00
4b	1860	None	*220,000*	20.00
1 Franc				
KF C 5a	1860	None	*100,000*	50.00
5b	1860	None	*160,000*	40.00
2 Francs				
KF C 6a	1860	None	*350,000*	$ 90.00
6b	1860	None	*400,000*	75.00
4 Francs				
KF C 7a	1860	None	*500,000*	175.00
7b	1860	None	*550,000*	150.00
10 Cents(Sen)				
KF C 8	1953	None	4,000,000	1.00
20 Cents(Sen)				
KF C 9	1953	None	3,000,000	1.25
50 Cents(Sen)				
KF C 10	1953	None	3,000,000	1.25

COIN — TOKEN

PHNOM PENH — ROYAL PALACE

10 Centimes				
KF CT 1	(1875)	None	*10,000*	10.00
15 Centimes				
KF CT 2	(1875)	None	*7,500*	15.00
20 Centimes				
KF CT 3	(1875)	None	*5,000*	20.00
25 Centimes				
KF CT 4	(1875)	None	*2,500*	25.00

PHNOM PENH — BUSINESS TOKEN

1 Centime				
KF CT 5	(1897)	None	*50,000*	7.50

NOTE — LEGAL TENDER

cty, code & number	(series) date	issued/ printed	high block	high serial	(EF) value
1 Piastre(Riel)					
KF N 1	(1952)	*1,000,000*	A.	00395066	$20.00
1 Piastre(Riel)					
KF N 2	(1953)	*25,000,000*	S10	024248900	7.50
5 Piastres(Riel)					
KF N 3	(1953)	*75,000,000*	C.29	565237	7.50
10 Piastres(Riel)					
KF N 4	(1953)	*5,000,000*	Q2	004062077	12.50
100 Piastres(Riel)					
KF N 5	(1953)	*19,000,000*	J.8	018344413	35.00
200 Piastres(Riel)					
KF N 6	(1953)	*2,500,000*	G.94	002331107	75.00

FRENCH LAOS

COIN — LEGAL TENDER

cty, code & number	date	mint mark	issued/ minted	(UNC) value
10 Cents(Att)				
LF C 1	1952	None	2,000,000	$1.00
20 Cents(Att)				
LF C 2	1952	None	3,000,000	1.00
50 Cents(Att)				
LF C 3	1952	Nonc	1,400,000	1.50

NOTE — LEGAL TENDER

cty, code & number	(series) date	issued/ printed	high block	high serial	(EF) value
1 Piastre(Kip)					
LF N 1	(1952)	*3,250,000*	A.	03122878	$20.00
1 Piastre(Kip)					
LF N 2	(1953)	*6,000,000*	F3	005587445	7.50
5 Piastres(Kip)					
LF N 3	(1953)	*65,000,000*	W.26	080048	10.00
10 Piastres(Kip)					
LF N 4	(1953)	*3,500,000*	J2	003338866	5.00
100 Piastres(Kip)					
LF N 5	(1953)	*20,000,000*	X.8	019662255	15.00

FRENCH VIET NAM

COIN — LEGAL TENDER

cty, code & number	(series) date	mint mark	issued/ minted	(UNC) value
Sapeque				
VF C 1	1905	None	60,000,000	$11.00
10 SU(Xu)				
VF C 2	1953	None	20,000,000	1.00
20 SU(Xu)				
VF C 3	1953	None	15,000,000	$1.00
50 XU				
VF C 4	1953	None	15,000,000	2.50

COIN — TOKEN

TRANG DA — SOCIETE MINIERE

cty, code & number	(series) date	mint mark	issued/ minted	(UNC) value
12 Sapeques				
VF CT 1	(1919)	None	*35,000*	4.50
15 Sapeques				
VF CT 2	(1919)	None	*30,000*	6.00
17 Sapeques				
VF CT 3	(1919)	None	*25,000*	7.50
25 Sapeques				
VF CT 4	(1919)	None	*20,000*	9.00
30 Sapeques				
VF CT 5	(1919)	None	*15,000*	11.50
35 Sapeques				
VF CT 6	(1919)	None	*10,000*	12.00

NOTE — LEGAL TENDER

cty, code & number	(series) date	issued/ printed	high block	high serial	(UNC) value
1 Piastre(Dong)					
VF N 1	(1952)	*5,000,000*	A.	42169470	$ 2.50
1 Piastre(Dong)					
VF N 2	(1953)	*115,000,000*	W44	109922845	2.50
5 Piastres(Dong)					
VF N 3	(1953)	*80,000,000*	N.31	782907	3.00
10 Piastres(Dong)					
VF N 4	(1953)	*60,000,000*	C.24	057766651	5.00
100 Piastres(Dong)					
VF N 5	(1953)	*26,000,000*	U.11	025028370	15.00
200 Piastres(Dong)					
VF N 6	(1953)	*21,000,000*	T.810	020243646	45.00

THAILAND(FRENCH)

COIN — TOKEN

cty, code & number	(series) date	mint mark	issued/ mintage	(EF) value
		MINES DE KHAOTREE		
2 ATT				
TF CT 1a	(1874)	None	*7,500*	$7.50
TF CT 1b	(1874)	None	*7,500*	7.50
TF CT 1c	(1874)	None	*7,500*	7.50

NOTE — TOKEN

cty, code & number	(series) date	issued/ printed	high block	high serial	(VF) value
	BANQUE DE L'INDOCHINE				
5 TICALS(Baht)					
TF NT 1	(1898)	*25,000*	—	—	$500.00
S1	19 Dec 98	*25*	o.0	000	250.00
20 TICALS(Baht)					
TF NT 2	(1898)	*50,000*	—	—	400.00
S2	(1898)	*25*	o.0	000	250.00
80 TICALS(Baht)					
TF NT 3	(1898)	*35,000*	—	—	600.00
S3	(1898)	*25*	o.0	000	250.00
100 TICALS(Baht)					
TF NT 4	(1898)	*25,000*	—	—	700.00
S4	7 Nov 98	*25*	o.0	000	250.00

NETHERLANDS EAST INDIES(FRENCH)

COIN — TOKEN

cty, code & number	date	mint mark	issued/ mintage	(VF) value
		G. DE MONTBRUN & CO.		
20 Cents				
IF CT 1	—	None	*7,500*	$3.00
50 Cents				
IF CT 2	—	None	*5,000*	5.00
1 Dollar				
IF CT 3	—	None	*2,500*	10.00
		SOCIETE DES TABACS DE DELI		
20 Cents				
IF CT 4	—	None	*7,500*	3.00
1 Dollar				
IF CT 5	—	None	2,500	10.00

BIBLIOGRAPHY

Altz, Charles G. and Barton, E.H., *Foreign Coins Struck at U.S. Mints,* Racine, 1965.
American Numismatic Association, *The Numismatist,* Monroe, Wichita, and Colorado Springs, various issues.
Amos Press, *Coin World* (newspaper) and *World Coins* (magazine), Sidney, various issues.
Blanchard, Wendell, *Thailand, Its People, Its Society, Its Culture,* New Haven, 1970.
Claude, Edmond, *Viet-Nam, Past and Present,* Saigon, 1957.
Davenport, John S., *The Dollars of Africa, Asia & Oceania,* Galesburg, 1969.
Do Van Minh, *Viet-Nam, Where East and West Meet,* New York, 1968.
Dobby, E.H.G., *Southeast Asia,* London, 1964.
Edmonds, I.G., *The Khmers of Cambodia,* New York, 1970.
Eklund, O.P., *Copper Coins of France,* Spokane, 1931.
Fairbank, Reischauser, and Craig, *East Asia, The Modern Transformation,* Tokyo, 1965.
Fall, Bernard B., *The Two Viet-Nams,* New York, 1967.
Gadoury, Victor, *Monnaies Francaise,* Baden-Baden, 1973 & 1977.
Guilloteau, V., *Monnaies Francaise 1670 - 1942,* Versailles, 1942.
Harris, Robert P., *A Guidebook of Modern European Coins,* Racine, 1965.
Hunter, John, *Price Catalog of Pure Nickel Coins of the World,* Chicago, 1969.
International Bank Note Society, *I.B.N.S. Journal,* Huntingdon, various issues.
Keller, Dr. Arnold, *Das Papiergeld des Ersten Weltkriegs, Teil II. Ubersee,* Berlin, 1957.
Kenny, Richard D., *Unofficial Coins of the World,* Chicago, 1964.
Krause, Chester L., and Mishler, Clifford, *Standard Catalog of World Coins,* Iola, 1974 & 1977.
Krause Publications, *World Coin News* (newspaper), Iola, various issues.
Lacroix, Desire, *Numismatique Annamite,* Paris, 1900.
Lamb, Robert A., *A Catalogue of French Emergency Tokens of 1914 - 1922,* Tuscon, 1967.
LeBau, Frank M., and Suddard, Adrienne, *Laos,* New Haven, 1960.
Lepczyk, Joseph, L., *Public Auction & Mail Bid Sale Catalogs,* East Lansing, various issues.
Loeb, Dr. Walter M., *Catalog of Paper Money Around the World,* Port Washington, 1961.
Mazard, Jean, *Historic Monetaire et Numismatique des Colonies et de l'Union Francaise,* Paris, 1953.
National Geographic Society, *National Geographic Magazine,* Washington, D.C., various issues.
Navy, Department of, *Indo-China,* Cambridge, 1943.
Nghiem, Dang, *Vietnam Politics and Public Administration,* Honolulu, 1966.
Numismatics International, *Numismatic International Bulletin,* Dallas, various issues.
Oka, M., *Silver Crowns of the Far East,* Tokyo, 1966.
Peters, Jess, *Mail Bid Sale Auction Catalogs,* Decatur, various issues.
Pick, Albert, *Standard Catalog of World Paper Money,* Iola, 1975 & 1977.
Randall, James P., *A Catalog of Foreign Silver and Copper Coins,* Fort Lauderdale, undated.
Raymond, Wayte, *France and Colonies,* New York, 1956.
Robequain, Charles, *The Economic Development of French Indochina,* New York, 1944.
Rolland, H., *Etude Numismatique sur le Protectorat du Cambodge,* Paris, 1932.
Sandrock, J.E., *World Paper Money Collection,* 1959.
Schroeder, Albert, *Annam, Etudes Numismatiques,* Paris, 1905.
Schulman Coin and Mint, *Fixed Price Lists,* New York, various issues.
Schulman, J., *Collection of Henry Thomas Grogan,* Amsterdam, 1914.
Schwan, C.F., and Boling, J.E., *World War II Military Currency,* Portage, 1978.
Scott, J.W., *Coins of the World, Standard Catalogues No. 1 & 2,* 1913 & 1916.
Semans, Scott, *World Coin Lists,* Oberlin and Cleveland, various issues.
Silvestre, J., *Monnaies et Medailles de l'Annam et de la Cochinchine Francaise,* Saigon, 1883.
Slabaugh, Arlie R., *Japanese Invasion Money,* Chicago, 1963.
Sten, George J., *Encyclopedia of World Paper Money,* Port Washington, 1965.
Superior Stamp & Coin Co., *Gilhousen Auction Sale - Part 2,* Los Angeles, 1973.
Thimonier, Argus, *Monnaies et Billets de Necessite 1914 - 1923,* Clermont-Ferrand, 1973.
Toy, Raymond S., and Meyer, Bob, *World War II Axis Military Currency,* Tuscon, 1967.
Tran, Tan Quoc, *Duoc Nha Nam, Dac Biet Tien,* Saigon, 1971.
Truong Chinh, *Primer for Revolt,* New York, 1963.
Uhl, Ted, *Fixed Price* and *Mail Auction Sale Lists,* Glen Burie and Auburndale, various issues.
Weyl Adolph, *Der Jules Fonrobertischen Sammlung,* Berlin, 1878.
World Paper Currency Collectors, *The Currency Collector* and *Newsletter,* Menlo Park, various issues.
Yeoman, Richard S., *A Catalog of Modern World Coins,* Racine, 1972.
　　　　　, *Current Coins of the World,* Racine, 1972.
Yongbungerd, Chalrum, *Account of Thai Bank Notes* (30th Anniversary), Bangkok, 1972.
Zay, E., *Histoire Monetaire des Colonies Francaise,* Paris, 1904.